WHITETAILS

Behavior ▪ *Natural History* ▪ *Conservation*

TEXT BY ERWIN A. BAUER
PHOTOGRAPHS BY ERWIN AND PEGGY BAUER

VOYAGEUR PRESS

TO THE FOLLOWING WHITETAIL FRIENDS:
Charles Alsheimer, Hefner Appling, Dick Buchonis, Vanny Cook, Cotton and Margaret Ellis, the Fossil Rim Wildlife Center, Gill Gigstead, Gordon Gillam, Allen Grimland, Bill Hendershot, Roy Hindes, George Jambers Jr., Clarence Johnstone, Robert King, Kermit Klaerner, Glenn Lau, George Laycock, John Leyendecker, Joe Linduska, Karl Maslowski, Bill Moody, John Moxley, Murphy Ray, Bob and Ann Reagan, Frank Rooke III, Lenny Rue III, Whitey Ryals, Frank and Homer Sayers, Charles Shreiner and the YO Ranch staff, Lloyd Shofner, Edwin Singer, Ed Vittetoe, Larry Weishuhn, the Rob and Bessie Welder Wildlife Foundation, and Russ White.
But most of all to Murry and Jolene Burnham.

Book designed by Lou Gordon ■ Cover designed by Leslie Dimond
Printed in Hong Kong
93   94   95   96   97   5   4   3   2   1

Library of Congress Cataloging-in-Publication Data
Bauer, Erwin A.
    Whitetails : behavior, ecology, and conservation / text by Erwin A. Bauer : photographs by Erwin and Peggy Bauer.
        p.   cm.
    Includes bibliographical references (p. 155) and index
    ISBN 0-89658-196-9
    1. White-tailed deer.   I. Bauer, Peggy.   II. Title
QL737.U55B388   1993
599.73'57—dc20   93-17728
                                      CIP

Published by VOYAGEUR PRESS, INC.
P.O. Box 338, 123 North Second Street, Stillwater, MN 55082 U.S.A.

Please write or call, or stop by, for our free catalog of natural history publications. Our toll-free number to place an order or to obtain a free catalog is 800-888-9653, or phone 612-430-2210 from Minnesota and Canada.

Educators, fundraisers, premium and gift buyers, publicists, and marketing managers:
Looking for creative products and new sales ideas? Voyageur Press books are available at special discounts when purchased in quantities, and special editions can be created to your specifications. For details contact the marketing department.

CONTENTS

THE WHITETAIL: NORTH AMERICA'S DEER　　7
The Evolution of the Whitetail ■ The Shifting Range of the Whitetail ■
The Whitetail's Physical Characteristics ■ The Senses of the Whitetail ■ Do
Whitetails Have a Home Range? ■ The Elusive and Vigorous Whitetail

THE LIFE HISTORY　　27
Autumn ■ Winter ■ Spring, Summer, and Foraging for the Return of Fall

THE BEHAVIOR OF A WHITETAIL　　59
From Play to Aggression ■ The Moon, the Rain, and the Wind ■ Does a
Whitetail use Body Language? ■ Older—and Wiser? ■ Diseases and Parasites
that Affect Deer ■ Do Humans Affect the Whitetail's Behavior?

ANTLERS　　73
How do Whitetails grow Antlers? ■ The Necessity of Antlers ■ Antlers for
Whitetail Admirers ■ Hunting for Trophies
■ Has Trophy-Hunting Gone Too Far?

WILDLIFE OF THE WHITETAIL'S WORLD　　99
Wolves and Whitetails ■ The "Deer Cat" ■ Coyotes
■ Black Bears and Bobcats ■ Observing the Whitetail's World

OTHER NORTH AMERICAN DEER　　123
Mule and Blacktailed Deer ■ Elk or Wapiti ■ Moose
■ Caribou ■ Exotic Deer

CONSERVATION AND THE FUTURE　　141
A Loved—and Loathed?—Animal ■ The Whitetail's Future

REFERENCES AND SUGGESTED READINGS　　155
INDEX　　156

THE WHITETAIL: NORTH AMERICA'S DEER

LaSalle County, south Texas. It is a penetrating, cold pre-dawn just before Christmas. I park my pickup where a narrow, rutted jeep track dead-ends in dense, brittle brush. Turning off the headlights, the car heater, and the engine, I sit listening for a moment. The only sound I hear is a north wind whining, driving dry pellets of snow.

Stepping outside into total darkness is a shock, and I shiver. The snow bites my face. Picking up a camera and tripod, shouldering a backpack full of accessories and a pair of discarded deer antlers, I follow a thin game trail into the brush. I try to travel quietly but it is impossible because my pack scrapes against mesquite branches and I stumble. Only the fact that I have often followed this same trail in bright daylight keeps me from losing my way to a blind I had built a week before.

My blind is a simple hiding place of natural vegetation, built low to the ground and woven between two clumps of prickly pear cacti. It is designed to blend into the surroundings and is located beside a clearing. The blind is just large enough to shield one person—me—in a sitting or crouched position with antlers on my lap. Although I cannot see them now, I know that fresh tracks of many whitetailed deer and the ground scrape of a large buck are etched in the earth near and all around the blind. A folding seat is inside; a narrow opening slits the natural brush at camera level. On hands and knees I enter and set up my camera and telephoto lens on a tripod.

Time passes in slow motion. A lemon light illuminates the eastern sky and, shivering again, I try to retreat farther into my insulated parka, stuffing cold hands deeper into the pockets. The lemon sky turns to gray, then white; now, the shadows that materialize beyond the clearing and the driven snow become deer. Does. The nearest pauses, stares in my direction, appears unalarmed at what she sees, and that is a good sign. Suddenly I'm no longer cold. The snow, but not the wind, stops.

The does browse and keep moving, facing into the wind, but they do not even look up when the shrill, haunting chorus of a coyote family carries from the distance. A few minutes later, I check my exposure meter and find that thanks to the powdery snow on the ground, which acts as a reflector, there is now minimum light for photography.

I pick up the deer antlers, crash them together hard, scrape them on the ground, then rattle the tines to imitate the sound of bucks fighting head to head. This time of year is the peak of the rut—the annual breeding season when combat is common in this part of Texas. I stop the rattling and sit quietly to listen for a response for several minutes, but no male deer comes to my challenge.

Picking up the antlers again, I crack them together once, scrape, pause, and then see movement just beyond the clearing through my camera slit. An instant later I notice the ivory tips of antlers poking above the brush and know it is a male deer. The only sound I hear now is my own pulse pounding.

I turn the camera ever so slowly in the deer's direction, and as I do, it bounds forward out into the open directly in front of the blind. There it stands motionless, head erect and ears forward. Its neck is swollen, its eyes alert; he is eager with

The whitetail is a graceful, durable, agile animal that is swift afoot and capable of living in many environments. This buck is Odocoileus virginianus texanus, *the Texas subspecies.*

the rut. Puzzled, it looks for an adversary it cannot see. The animal has the massive rack—antlers—of a very large deer, possibly the largest I have ever seen.

I try to bring the deer into focus in my viewfinder, and squeeze the shutter. The metallic sound of the motor drive seems to shock the deer into action. It shudders and snorts once. I squeeze off another exposure and then the clearing is empty. The great buck has vanished as suddenly as it appeared. For a few moments I sit in wonder and amazement.

THE EVOLUTION OF THE WHITETAIL

During a lifetime devoted to hunting wildlife around the world with a camera, that brief minute with the magnificent south Texas whitetail on a gray December morning remains among my most indelible of memories. Even though my wife Peggy and I have focused on everything from wild geese to grizzly bears, from hummingbirds to hyenas and African rhinos, and even though my two pictures of that Texas buck were not sharp and were poorly exposed, I will never forget that encounter.

Most hunters will understand. They agree that the whitetail deer is the most challenging, perhaps the greatest big game species in North America, if not on earth. Even more, nonhunters regard this animal among the handsomest, most noble of our native wildlife, as a perfect symbol of wildness, natural beauty, and of our precious outdoors that is too fast draining away.

But exactly what is the whitetailed deer, *Odocoileus virginianus*, this animal that is so admired and beloved? Numbering between twenty and twenty-five million in the early 1990s, it is by far the most abundant large mammal in the New World, perhaps on all the earth. It is also among the most resilient and adaptable, being able to survive (if not actually to thrive) in wilderness as well as where the human population continues to increase and change the face of the land. It lives in deserts and wetlands, in mountains and on prairies, in intense cold and terrible heat. But in one sense, it is not really a native. Of all North American hooved animals, only the pronghorn, musk ox, and javelina (or collared peccary) originated on this continent. All of the North American deer (moose, elk, caribou, and mule deer as well as whitetails) are among the immigrants that wandered eastward over a land bridge that connected Asia to Alaska fifteen million years ago.

Going back even further than that, we now know from fossil remains that the agile, graceful whitetail evolved from some piglike ancestor that stood less than two feet high. That always seems hard to believe until the similarities between deer and swine today are considered. More than once in the southeastern United States woodlands (where both live) I've had trouble telling the split, cloven hoofprints of whitetails from those of wild hogs. Both mammals have compact bodies and elongated skulls, as well as short, stiff body hair. In structure their legs are similar, except that a deer's legs are longer. The two share a keen sense of smell.

Consider some other similarities. Whenever domestic hogs escape and run wild, they prefer the same habitat as whitetails. Both live on highly varied diets and are in turn among the most favored prey of such predators as the wild cats and wild dogs. Neither deer nor pigs sweat profusely when pursued or during great physical exertion. Maybe the most surprising of all is that their vocalizations are remarkably similar. Both bark, grunt, squeal, and snort, although deer less often than pigs.

As interesting as comparisons to pigs may be, we must keep in mind that whitetails have much more in common with the other ruminants, or cud-chewing mammals, than with pigs. During the thousands of centuries since their arrival in North America, the factors of the environment (including the vegetation and often harsh weather), plus pressure from predators, has created the modern elusive and physiologically tough whitetail we know today.

Scientifically, the generic name *whitetail* really refers to thirty different races, or subspecies, of deer that taxonomists have historically recognized, although that number of subspecies is—these days—challenged. Whitetails inhabit almost every region of the North American continent (except Baja and southern California, Alaska, and Arctic Canada) from Panama north to Quebec and southernmost Yukon. With a few exceptions, the largest, heaviest deer are those living farthest north, while the smallest live farthest south. If both deer stand together, it is possible to tell one of the smallest, the Florida Key deer, *Odocoileus virginianus clavium*, which is no bigger than a foxhound or a collie, from any of the largest such as the prototype—the first subspecies recognized—Virginia or eastern whitetail, *Odocoileus virginianus virginianus*. But beyond that comparison, distinguishing one subspecies from another outside the laboratory is a difficult, perhaps impossible matter.

Four subspecies make up most of the North American population. These are *Odocoileus virginianus virginianus*, the Virginia whitetail of the southeastern United States; *Odocoileus virginianus borealis*, the northeastern whitetail, which ranges into Quebec and Ontario; *Odocoileus virginianus macrouras* of

The North and Central American Range of the Whitetailed Deer (*Odocoileus virginianus*) by Subspecies

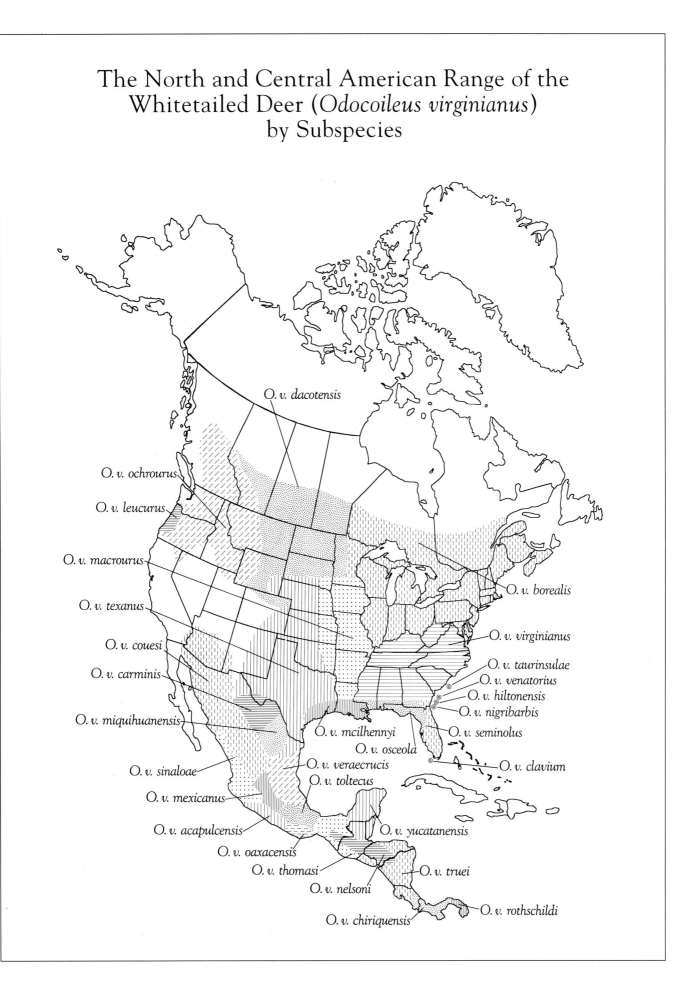

O. v. dacotensis

O. v. ochrourus

O. v. leucurus

O. v. macrourus

O. v. texanus

O. v. couesi

O. v. carminis

O. v. miquihuanensis

O. v. sinaloae

O. v. mexicanus

O. v. acapulcensis

O. v. oaxacensis

O. v. thomasi

O. v. nelsoni

O. v. chiriquensis

O. v. mcilhennyi

O. v. osceola

O. v. veraecrucis

O. v. toltecus

O. v. yucatanensis

O. v. truei

O. v. rothschildi

O. v. borealis

O. v. virginianus

O. v. taurinsulae

O. v. venatorius

O. v. hiltonensis

O. v. nigribarbis

O. v. seminolus

O. v. clavium

Above: *The Ozarks of central Missouri.* **Right:** *The Everglades in southern Florida.*

The range in which whitetails now live throughout the United States and all across southern Canada is tremendous, as is the diversity of habitat. Whitetails live from Florida's Everglades to North Dakota's Theodore Roosevelt National Park, the Upper Peninsula of Michigan to southwestern Texas's Big Bend National Park, the Ozarks in Missouri to the Paradise Valley in Montana, and the farmlands of the Midwest to the banks of Mississippi's rivers.

Theodore Roosevelt National Park in North Dakota.

The Upper Peninsula of Michigan.

Above: *Big Bend National Park, Texas.*
Left: *The Yazoo River in Mississippi.*

Paradise Valley in Montana.

Farmland in Ohio.

the Iowa bottomlands south to Louisiana; and *Odocoileus virginianus texanus* of Texas, Oklahoma, and Kansas.

But not everyone agrees with this grouping. In fact, none of these subspecies may really exist any longer, and many taxonomists never completely agreed on their classifications or geography anyway. Since about 1900, many government and private conservation agencies have tried to reestablish whitetails into areas of scarcity or to locally "improve the breed." Whitetails have been live-trapped, transported, and transshipped by the thousands back and forth across the country without regard to range or subspecies. As a result of interbreeding, most whitetails today are simply generic whitetails.

THE SHIFTING RANGE OF THE WHITETAIL

When the first Europeans colonized the eastern seaboard over three centuries ago, they found a nearly virgin paradise only sparsely inhabited by humans, but teeming with game. Some colonies might have failed without the wild turkeys, quail, grouse, and waterfowl, without the blizzards of shorebirds they found from Jamestown to Plymouth Rock. They also discovered another unfamiliar animal, the whitetailed deer. The native people, who helped to teach the Europeans how to live in this New World, relied heavily on the whitetail for both fresh and dried venison, and on its skin for jackets, mittens, moccasins, and leggings.

No part of this deer was wasted by the native peoples. The hide was tanned for drumheads and war shields and the rawhide thongs that went into snowshoes and bowstrings. Antlers became tools and weapons. Hooves were fashioned into rattles, pipes, and ceremonial gewgaws. Bones were boiled to season maize, hominy, and beans.

But the abundance of deer did not exist far beyond the eastern seaboard, until deliberate burning around Indian encampments and later clearing of the land by settlers produced

Left: *This is an extraordinary Texas buck; few readers will ever see one with antlers to match it either alive in the wild or pictured in a book.* **Overleaf:** *The Sierra del Carmen in Coahuila, Mexico, and the adjoining Chisos Mountains of Big Bend National Park, Texas, make up the range of the Carmen Mountains subspecies of whitetail (Odocoileus virginianus carminis). These were photographed against a passing winter storm, high above the Rio Grande River.*

This healthy, typical-looking northern whitetailed deer was photographed in early winter in Minnesota, near the Tamarac National Wildlife Refuge. Here is what northern and midwestern deer hunters dream about during the rest of the year.

an ideal local habitat for the deer. Most of the eastern United States and Canada was originally covered by vast, unbroken tracts of virgin timber where sunlight seldom penetrated to the forest floor. This was poor whitetailed deer environment. Deer thrived only along forest edges and in scattered openings. In fact, because of the changed landscape, there are far more whitetails living in all America today than when the Pilgrims waded ashore in Massachusetts.

At that time, we now believe, the range of the whitetail was mainly east of the Mississippi River valley, plus Texas and Mexico, south to Venezuela. The rest of North America was occupied by mule deer, *Odocoileus hemionus*, a slightly larger "cousin." But with westward expansion during the eighteenth century, more and more of the original eastern forest was cut. The combination of axe, plow, and fire with bushy regrowth gradually increased the amount of deer range from Boston and Baltimore all the way to Cincinnati, St. Louis, and beyond. So the population of whitetailed deer exploded in the wake of farmers and lumbermen. Mule deer probably retreated from some such areas. The boom lasted until a second wave of settlement (made possible by passage of the historic Homestead Act of 1862) swept farther westward from the East.

For the next half-century, whitetails were shot by market hunters for venison or simply to keep them out of croplands. The toll in some areas almost wiped out deer, and they never really recovered until the modern conservation practices and scientific game management following World War II were implemented. The last half-century has been the golden age of the whitetail, with the species ever expanding westward into traditional mule deer range. To date, deer researchers are baffled by this encroachment, which finds whitetails firmly established now in river valleys and lowlands from the Dakotas to Montana, and north into western Canada, where they are reaching a very large size for the species.

THE WHITETAIL'S PHYSICAL CHARACTERISTICS
Size and Weight

Deer measurements and weights vary greatly with range (northern animals weigh more than those in the southern part of their range), and of course with age. Bucks reach maximum body size at about four and one-half to five and one-half years. From then until they are eight and one-half years old or so, their antlers continue to grow (or be larger each fall) if their

The range of the whitetail extends southward even into South America. We photographed this small buck of the subspecies Odocoileus virginianus gymnotis *in Venezuela. Even in photographs, it is usually evident that the southern whitetails are smaller than their northern counterparts.*

diet is nutritious. Their overall body weight could continue to increase slightly until they are about ten or eleven years old, when their teeth wear out. Does grow heavier until they are four and one-half or five and one-half years old, but then begin a gradual decline even if their teeth are in good condition.

Whitetails vary in overall measurements as well. Rarely is the back of any adult deer higher than the belt buckle of a six-foot human. Northern deer average about forty inches high at the shoulder. Southern races may be only a little more than half that.

Mature males of the Coues subspecies (*Odocoileus virginianus couesi*) of southern Arizona and the Mexican state of Sonora rarely exceed one hundred pounds. I once weighed a "large" Carmen Mountains whitetail (*Odocoileus virginianus carminis*) buck of the Texas Big Bend country near the Rio Grande River that weighed only 105 pounds, even though it was six and one-half to seven and one-half years old—nearly its maximum age. It is interesting to note that these Carmen deer have oversized hooves to better travel through the rocky, cactus-infested Trans-Pecos region.

At the other extreme, two-hundred-pound-plus bucks cause very little excitement in most of the northern United States and southern Canada. I weighed one Ohio male whitetail at 214 pounds, field dressed—that is, with the entrails removed. During one 1970s deer study in that state, does averaged 138 pounds and the bucks about 180 pounds.

Some individual whitetailed deer reach prodigious size. A field-dressed Nebraska buck was officially listed at 310 pounds; it would have weighed 380 on the hoof. Maine's largest known buck weighed 355 pounds. New York Conservation Department officers once weighed a buck shot near Mud Lake in the Adirondacks at 388 pounds. Perhaps the giant of all, the United States record, was a Michigan male, which with entrails removed and blood drained still weighed 354 on

honest scales. Its live weight would have been about 425 pounds. By contrast, a fully grown whitetailed buck living on Coiba Island, Panama, might not weigh fifty pounds.

The Canadian and world record whitetail may have been the super-buck shot between Lakes Huron and Erie near London, Ontario, in 1977 by archer John Annett. It weighed 196 kilos (or 431 pounds) on government-inspected balance beam scales. Unfortunately Annett field dressed and skinned this animal before provincial conservation officials could examine it.

This Columbian whitetail buck (Odocoileus virginianus leucurus) of tidelands and coastal forests in western Oregon and Washington is one of thirty subspecies in North America. Only a few hundred Columbians survive, mostly on state refuges.

Pelage

Summertime whitetails wear reddish tan, lightweight, warm-weather coats for about three months in the north part of their range, or four months elsewhere. The rest of the time they have heavier, grayish tan winter coats that may seem blue in a dark autumn woods. After re-examining the deer color photos we have made over the past quarter-century throughout whitetail range, the seasonal coats appear to differ much less in southern than in northern whitetails. The animals of Texas and the central American plains tend to be the most pale. The darkest whitetails by far are those of the northern woodlands.

Summer coats have little bulk; to better cope with warm, sometimes hot weather, the deer have only light underhair beneath the coarse, red, outer hair. By September almost everywhere, the summer pelage is shed in favor of winter gray. The new hairs are hollow, stiff, and about two inches long in the north, and shorter in the south. Underneath, softer hair curls closely against the skin. This is enough insulation to keep a whitetail warm as its beds down in snow for long periods, perhaps for the duration of a storm, without appreciably thawing the snow on which the animal lies.

No matter what the season, every whitetail has a white patch on its throat, a white or off-white belly, and white in-

Elusive whitetails blend well into their habitats throughout the year. We managed to locate and photograph this buck in dense cattails surrounding an Iowa farm pond, where it felt secure.

side each leg. Also there is white inside the hairy ears, around the eyes, and on the chin, which is marked with a black spot on the lower jaw.

But the twelve- to fifteen-inch-long tail is the animal's trademark, for which it is named. Brown on the outside, but pure white underneath, too often the waving pennant-shaped tail is all anyone sees of a shy deer departing for a jackpine thicket or other dense cover. Does much more often than males raise and wave their tails when either alarmed or running away. This may enable fawns to more easily see and follow their mothers in times of danger. No wonder that the species is also known regionally as the fantail or flagtail.

THE SENSES OF THE WHITETAIL

Every whitetail is born with splendid hearing, with a phenomenal sense of smell, and good eyesight even in semidarkness. With senses like these, the species does not need to be smart.

Hearing and Communication

Studies have revealed that a whitetail's hearing is so acute that it can instantly distinguish the footfall of a bear or of a human from that of another deer without bothering to look up. That information is transmitted to the brain, and if the sound is bruin or human, the deer, without having to think at all, is programmed to bolt. From long observation I realize that a whitetail may not show any visible sign that it knows a person is approaching. But it *is* aware and ready to flee nonetheless.

It is interesting and revealing to watch a deer's ears. When one points forward and the other backward, the animal is simply checking the way ahead while keeping track of its backtrail and whatever may be following. By constantly "focusing" or "tuning in" its large ears in all directions, a whitetail remains aware of its surroundings and any activities taking place. In this way, a doe always knows the exact location of its fawn and of other does in the herd.

Field research has shown that a deer can hear another whitetail walking in heavy brush from as far as fifty yards away and, because a human may be louder (or may give off olfactory clues), a human farther than that. The sound of another deer's movement is either reassuring or alarming, depending on the pace. A slow speed is normally reassuring, but the sound of a fast moving deer can be cause for alarm—the deer is running away from something. Even the careful mincing step of a whitetailed doe seems to have two purposes: The delicate step is less alarming to other deer, and it does not cancel out

other common woodland sounds. When both a whitetail's ears are laid down flat behind the head, it is frightened and ready to flush. The deer may hold its ears this way to prevent injury to this vital and delicate mechanism when bounding wildly through heavy cover. Flattened ears may also signal annoyance, such as another deer approaching too near.

Whitetails communicate with one another by a variety of sounds. Both sexes, but especially females, stamp their feet when puzzled by an object, a person, or another animal they can see but cannot yet identify. The reason may be to make the mystery move and reveal itself. Fawns bleat softly to keep contact with mothers. Males and females snort to warn of danger. A buck grunting is usually one that is trailing a doe in heat, and it will sneeze to threaten another buck that comes too close during the pursuit of love. I have also heard other sounds from wheezing and whining to raspy grunting, most often during the rutting season or when competing for limited food.

Smell

Whitetails have metatarsal glands on the outsides of both hind legs, and these secrete an alarm scent when the animal suddenly comes under stress, an odor that is unpleasant to humans. Other deer nearby are thus warned by this olfactory message, often from a great distance if the wind is favorable. It is probably easy for some predators to smell and realize instantly that a deer has recently departed the vicinity. The wet nose of a deer increases its keen sense of smell because pheromones—scent particles—stick to the moisture longer.

Vision

Although keen, a deer's vision is monocular rather than binocular or three-dimensional, like a human's. A human being with good peripheral vision can accurately see things within 160 to 170 degrees of a circle when focused on an object straight ahead. As a prey species with eyes on opposite sides of the head, a whitetail can detect motion 300 to 310 degrees of a circle (or all but directly behind it) when looking straight ahead. But vision of the deer's two eyes overlaps only fifteen degrees or less when a deer looks forward, accounting for its near monocular vision.

Although a deer can look straight ahead at a completely motionless man and not notice him, that same animal can immediately spot unnatural movement—in fact *any* slight movement—from a considerable distance and anywhere except directly behind. Such movements, as much as anything,

The face of a whitetailed doe is framed in the lush, deep vegetation of summer. Note especially the alert, "tuned-in" ears. All whitetails have extraordinary hearing.

alert a deer to the presence or approach of danger. Keep in mind that a deer may go through a charade of not seeing, of continuing to eat or walk slowly, but still know that a person is near or something is not exactly right.

DO WHITETAILS HAVE A HOME RANGE?

Although deer behavior varies somewhat from region to region, depending on habitat type, hunting pressure, and other factors, some broad statements can be said about typical or average behavior. Deer seem to know very well the area or home range they frequent, probably where they were born, especially all of its escape routes. Although this species does not establish and defend territories from other deer, scientific studies in different localities indicate that bucks especially have definite core areas of from forty to one hundred acres in which they spend three-fourths of their time. When they do leave, it is the temporary search for greener pastures to forage or to breed.

Radio tracking has shown that, year-round, does wander more than bucks and in a more random fashion. Bucks tend to travel on the shortest, straightest path, for example, between bedding and feeding areas. One researcher, who examined countless trails and hoofprints very closely, decided that most does tend to walk pigeon-toed while bucks turn hooves slightly outward, maybe because of their heavier body weight. Males with widespread antlers opt to walk around dense cover rather than through it unless they are being pursued.

THE ELUSIVE AND VIGOROUS WHITETAIL

The brain of a whitetail is smaller relative to body size and much smoother than a human's, two indications that deer are not very intelligent. Most hunters may find that hard to accept. In fact, deer are dimwitted compared to coyotes, foxes, raccoons, the wild cats, birds of prey, and even the feral pigs that share their habitat. Apparently they cannot count and have such short memories that often they cannot recall, only a few minutes after a severe fright, what alarmed them in the first place. Many times I've watched whitetails bound away in terror only to stop and calmly browse five minutes later and less than a mile away. But keep in mind that innate shyness, suspicion, and the keenest of survival instincts more than compensate for any lack of genuine intelligence.

Whitetails are so shy, in fact, that they exist almost anonymously in many communities. I've visited places where human residents did not know that deer existed among them, sometimes just beyond their backyards, until a few animals were killed along the highways or by dogs, or were spotted along roadsides in the beams of headlights at night.

Perhaps the most outstanding characteristic of a whitetail, especially of an older one, is its ability to move quietly, ghostlike over its territory and to practically dissolve into its environment, no matter whether desert or balsam swamp, winter or summer. Far too often I have found myself looking directly at deer yet not seeing them for long moments. Few animals are better escape artists than these.

Few if any of the world's large mammals are equipped with as many efficient escape or survival mechanisms as the adult whitetailed deer. First, here is one very prolific species that can outproduce its natural enemies. A whitetail's winter coat blends well into a gray December woods for camouflage. Very fast afoot, any whitetail is also a lithe and powerful jumper, and a beautiful spectacle to see. When healthy it is easily able to outdistance any natural predators over deadfalls and through the most terrible terrain. With a running start, effortless bounds of over twenty-five feet are not unusual and when alarmed, whitetails will jump over farm or ranch fences to escape. However, in some areas they prefer to crawl under them. No other American hoofed animal can vanish from sight so swiftly and so gracefully. Only the native pronghorn antelope is faster afoot. I submit that nobody realizes these points so well as a professional wildlife photographer who has been stalking all kinds of big game for most of his life, and not often enough with great success.

Far too frequently a deer's great leaps have been too fast to follow with a camera, let alone for the shutter to absolutely freeze. Too many pictures of whitetailed bucks in flight have been only horizontal blurs on the color slides because of the difficulty of both following and focusing sharply on such a swift subject. (Recently the introduction of automatic focus cameras has improved our results.) But what makes this species truly unique is that, despite the frail-looking, thin limbs, and no matter how rapidly it is running, a deer can stop abruptly and race immediately away in an entirely different direction, a maneuver that would seem to shatter its front legs. This feat is possible because the whitetail's forelegs do not connect directly to the skeleton. Rather, they are separated by a tough, resistant cartilage that serves as a heavy-duty shock absorber.

The entire musculature and skeleton of a whitetail are meant for running over uneven terrain. To make good an escape, whitetails have two classic gaits: trotting and galloping. When trotting, they look forward with the head and tail held erect, the tail wagging from side to side. The gallop, which

The whitetail is a great escape artist, able to quickly dissolve into its habitat at any time of year. Streams are no barriers to escape.

is most beautiful to see, mixes long strides with graceful leaps that can clear obstacles as high as eight feet. Top running speed is about thirty-five miles per hour. A startled whitetail can jump a six-foot obstacle from a standing start.

To simply state that the animal that many consider gentle, frail, defenseless, and Bambi-like is instead tough and tenacious is certainly an understatement. Here is a species able to endure incredibly harsh conditions, extremes of heat and cold, and (more recently) environmental degradation of its habitat. The toughening process begins at the moment of conception during the annual rut, probably at night in a bleak and frosty forest glade.

Today's whitetail is a product of the stresses and strains of fifteen million years of evolution, since the Miocene Period when it arrived and spread across our continent. Somehow the whitetails managed to survive the great glaciers and the droughts that periodically gripped North America and eliminated less adaptable, less rugged species such as mastodons and sabertoothed cats. Our modern whitetail endured incredible climatic changes as well as a changing cast of predators, plus the human exploitation of more recent times, to be the durable and handsome creature we admire.

One scientific experiment, this one on the Upper Penin-

sula of Michigan in 1965, demonstrated very well the extreme shyness and durability of the whitetail. State wildlife officials stocked thirty-nine whitetailed deer into an escape-proof, ten-foot-high cyclone-fenced enclosure of the Cusino Wildlife Experiment Station, which was only one square mile in size. The habitat inside the enclosure was typical of northern Michigan's whitetail habitat. Nine of the thirty-nine confined deer were bucks. During favorable weather and with a fresh tracking snow on the ground, six experienced hunters were allowed to hunt freely within the area.

This happened at about the same time that Walt Disney's popular film "Bambi" was showing across America, and a new antihunting movement was beginning to form. More than one well-known newspaper columnist sneered at the Cusino experiment as very unsporting to hunt any deer, let alone those trapped inside a ten-foot fence. It is understandable that it stirred a good bit of public indignation.

But here are the facts. Four days elapsed before any of the six hunters even glimpsed one of the nine bucks. And a total of fifty-one hunting hours passed before one buck was finally shot in this confinement. It is remarkable testimony to the wiliness of a remarkable wild animal. The whitetail is no Bambi.

THE LIFE HISTORY

AUTUMN

Usually late autumn is the most exciting, the busiest, the most dramatic time in the lives of white-

tailed deer everywhere. It is the rut, or breeding season, when bucks suddenly discard some of their normal caution to go out on the prod, looking for females. Does coming into estrus also begin searching for males.

For a long time, we believed that the rut was brought on by cold weather, by snow or falling leaves or by plunging temperatures, that unseasonably hot weather could delay the fall breeding season or that an early cold spell could hasten its arrival. But we now know that a phenomenon called photoperiodism is responsible. At a certain same time at a certain latitude every year, the waning light of fall gradually induces great hormonal changes in both sexes.

With the rut, the hormone balance in every buck's body changes and the blood supply to its now fully mineralized—hardened—antlers is cut off. Necks of some males swell by as much as ten inches in circumference. More blood is pumped into neck tissues, and muscle mass suddenly expands as a cushion during future fighting. The velvet antler covering dies and is either rubbed off or begins to peel away. A little later during the rut, one by one the does come into estrus.

Most of the year bucks are secretive, retiring, and far less social than does, who, with their fawns, associate in small bands. But with the rut, bachelor bucks become less cautious, more visible, and behave in a more aggressive and sexual manner. Early in the rut they go about rubbing antlers on trees, but not because of itching or to get rid of lingering loose velvet. These rubs, especially very fresh ones, are signs that bucks are or have been in a vicinity working off excess sexual energy or frustration. At the same time they are also scent marking with orbital glands near the eye. Most of the time younger males select small, whippy saplings for rubbing while larger deer use small trees.

Often at this time I have watched bucks graduate from simply rubbing to fighting trees and bushes. One frosty morning in Michigan, I witnessed a buck with ten-point antlers as it made a furious attack on a young balsam tree, start to walk away as if the winner, then return for another long round, completely defoliating the tree. Such attacks on imaginary rivals may help vent a buck's aggressions, as a kind of energy release valve in lieu of an encounter with another buck. Or it may simply serve as training for more serious bouts yet to come.

To Attract Does

Rutting bucks also make scrapes in bare earth, by pawing with forefeet, 80 to 90 percent of the time just under overhanging tree branches that can be hooked or twisted with antlers, or licked with the tongue. One deer biologist calculated that during the breeding period each buck makes about twenty-seven scrapes in which it paws away fallen leaves and debris. It then leaves its own scent on each scrape by urinating, defecating, or from secretions from the interdigital or foot glands. When urinating, the buck allows the urine to drip over the tarsal glands located on the insides of the hind legs. The vi-

Toward the end of autumn, whitetail bucks everywhere give up their sedentary summer lives and begin to explore, looking for the first signals of does coming into estrus. The bucks now make a lot more footprints and other sign as they travel over their territories.

cinities of scrapes are such obvious places to try to photograph large bucks that I have often waited nearby in blinds to ambush the deer. Sometimes it works.

A lovesick male may return as often as three times a day to check his own most recent scrape for any evidence of a doe in estrus nearby, attracted by the scrape. Some bucks seem to establish a necklace of scrapes across the landscape as a trapper establishes his trapline. Large bucks may make their own scrapes on top of those of lesser males.

Biologists disagree on how, or if, scrapes are related to buck territories. Nor do they agree whether scraping, as some observers in the Midwest insist, marks the limits of home areas. Summed up, scraping probably serves two purposes at the same time: attracting breeding females while intimidating male rivals.

The size of a scrape often indicates the age (and therefore the size) of the scraper. From my own experience, a saucer-sized scrape is usually the mark of an immature male. I figure that scrapes of dinner-plate size were usually left by medium or average bucks. I have found a few scrapes in Texas, Iowa, and Missouri of two to three feet in diameter; patient watching from a distance revealed that in all cases these really were signs of, probably, the largest bucks living in the area. On the other hand, one of the largest scrapes I have ever found was made by a small forkhorn (antlers with two points per side) buck on my own home place in Montana's Yellowstone Valley. Almost as much research has been done on deer scraping as on anything else except food and feeding habits. But the main point of agreement among the researchers is that scraping is interesting and important rut behavior.

Buck to Buck

In truth, fighting between bucks does not occur as often as is sometimes claimed, but does take place most frequently where bucks are either abnormally numerous or where the ratio of bucks to does is high. The rattle of antlers is much more likely to be heard over landscapes where there is one buck per doe than where does outnumber males five or more to one. Peggy and I have watched males clash on numerous occasions, and no two of these duels are exactly the same.

Some encounters end when, after barely brushing antlers, one buck seems intimidated just by the more impressive appearance of the other. More often it is a case of rivals circling

The rutting season in the central Texas Hill Country reveals some splendid bucks that are much more secretive at other times of the year. They are especially visible just after dawn and just before sunset.

and gauging each other, hair bristling, reddened eyeballs bulging, before joining in a crash and rattle that can be heard far away. Some of these clashes end quickly; others (if the deer are very evenly matched) become violent, lengthy fencing matches in which each tries to break through the other's defense. Sometimes the fur really does fly. A lot of forest turf may be torn up and deer hide may be punctured before the loser slinks away. It is quite common for the sound of this combat to attract other bucks to the scene.

The arena for the most violent rutting fight we have ever witnessed was on a south Texas ranch shortly after a cold late fall daybreak. Driving in an open jeep with rancher Cotton Ellis, I hit the brake when I spotted two splendid bucks lunging head to head in the track. The two seemed evenly matched for several minutes, but suddenly one flipped the other completely over onto its back and then tried to plunge antlers into its flank. Somehow the loser managed to regain its feet and run away. It seemed to be injured. But in the weeks following, Ellis daily searched that same vicinity but never again saw the vanquished deer dead or alive.

On a number of occasions I have watched very young bucks with only spike or small forked antlers fighting with as much intensity as their grandfathers. Although it amounts only to practice for the future, it is serious business for the contestants. I am amazed that more of these youngsters are not blinded by the sharp spikes of the other.

As angry as any deer fighting may seem, we do not know whether whitetail bucks fight to kill or inflict injury, or simply to send a rival away. Most of the time the damage and spoils are psychological. The winner retains his ground and rank; the loser walks away. Nor do bucks compete in battle with an expectant, ready doe standing nearby and awaiting the attentions of the winner as we often see in wildlife calendar paintings. The match is simply to decide which deer is stronger, more dominant, number one—which buck will do most of the breeding when that time soon comes. The average confrontation does not end in serious injury to either combatant. Any does in the vicinity do not even bother to watch, no matter how exciting the contest may seem to human observers.

Of course there are exceptions. I photographed a Montana whitetail that had lost an eye, most likely because of the season in a rutting action. Wildlife author John Madson wrote of a five-year-old buck that had forty-seven antler punctures in its skin and that may have died from these wounds. In Louisiana a buck was found with an antler tine broken off and driven into its skull. Still, more bucks may perish from having their antlers become hopelessly locked when fighting than from any puncture injuries. But even this is not common. When locking does occur, both animals usually die slow deaths or are eaten by predators. But not always.

A northern Minnesota forester, Tom Swedlund, shot a buck with what seemed at a distance to be a strange and abnormally large rack of antlers. Approaching the animal, he was shocked to see that the rack and skull of another whitetail buck were entangled in its own antlers. The winner of a rutting season combat had somehow outlived its rival and managed to wrench its head from the carcass. Swedlund said his unique trophy was thin and emaciated, but probably would have survived because it would soon have shed both its own and the rival's antlers. A west Texas rancher found coyotes eating a dead deer that was still antler-locked to a very weak living buck.

Mating

Rutting bucks almost always initiate actual breeding. They do not acquire harems (as is often and incorrectly pictured), but freelance in pursuit of single does. Perhaps because the aura of oncoming estrus is there, bucks may follow still unreceptive does closely, relentlessly, driving away rivals, for as long as ten days until finally successful in mating or until a more powerful buck takes over the pursuit. Meanwhile, a pursued doe uses a whole catalog of evasions—such as running, sneaking, bedding down, seeking and mingling among other deer, even standing in a cold stream—to try to elude the persistent bucks.

When a doe does reach full estrus, which lasts only a day, she suddenly becomes less shy and allows herself to be caught. She advertises availability by extending her tail straight out behind and slightly to one side, while stepping nimbly with head upright. If unescorted, she may run and jump crazily to attract attention. The mating, which most often takes place at night, is quick and lacking in what humans might call tenderness. If for some reason a doe is not impregnated, another estrus season comes twenty-eight days later and this time, biologists have observed, females become much more aggressive and begin to actively pursue bucks. That may well be necessary, because after a month of frantic rutting activity when eating has been neglected, the most powerful bucks may have lost as much as a quarter of their accumulated body weight and with it much of their strength. The thrill and the will to breed are almost gone. The curtain of the rutting season finally slams down when bucks lose their antlers and overnight become as docile as does.

From a tree blind, we photographed this buck making a ground scrape with a forefoot along a trail he regularly patrols during the rut. Scrapes are an announcement or an advertisement of availability for breeding.

With the arrival of late autumn, male whitetails emerge from heavier cover, where they spend most of summer daylight hours, to search for does in estrus. Along the way, they rub antlers on trees and brush, scent mark with preorbital glands and by licking, scrape the ground with hooves, and even uproot small saplings from the ground—all prerutting activities. **Right:** *This buck is seriously pursuing the doe's trail. Sometimes two or more bucks will converge in such tracking, and there will be a confrontation.*

Across the northern United States and in most of the whitetail's range in Canada, the rut peaks during the last half of November. Southern whitetails breed later. The peak in south Texas comes during the Christmas season and in Arizona it is a little later than that. Whitetailed deer in Latin America have no definite rutting season and may breed at any time. As one gets farther away from the Equator, the light cycles and thus the breeding cycles become more distinct. Scientists have discovered that deer moved from one geographical region to another usually soon adapt their breeding season to the new climate.

Photographing Whitetails in Autumn
The breeding season is the easiest and most exciting time to photograph whitetailed deer. Peggy and I try to be afield as much as possible during this period and many of the photos in this book are a result of it. The bucks especially are more predictable than at other times, and for a few weeks they are much less shy. Innate caution is tempered by the pursuit of love. We take advantage of that in a number of ways.

Rattling antlers to attract bucks into telephoto lens range is one tactic that has worked in about half the places we have tried it. The idea is to sound like two bucks fighting, an encounter that other bucks within hearing might investigate.

We have also often used tree blinds in the vicinity of buck scrapes, especially when the scrapes are made near frequently used deer trails. A number of fine, lightweight and portable, easy-to-erect tree blinds are available for this. In addition, we apply commercially made doe-in-rut scents to vegetation in the immediate vicinity, and at times this aura seems to have a magical effect. More than once I have watched bucks come eagerly upwind from far away to determine the source of the scent.

One of the finest bucks we have ever photographed was actually decoyed into point-blank camera range near Del Rio, Texas. Murry Burnham, who is probably the greatest of all wild game callers, had stretched the hide of a female deer over a wooden frame to make a fairly decent looking full-bodied decoy he called Dodo. We placed the counterfeit near a fresh buck scrape, doused it with scent, and retreated to a mesquite

blind nearby to wait. Within an hour two bucks came courting Dodo. The larger of the two was a magnificent animal that at one point almost filled my viewfinder.

Not all strategy works so well. On another occasion in Alberta, I climbed into a tree blind just before dawn. A number of deer trails converged near the tree and all around were signs of recent deer activity. I climbed up into the tree and once in place pulled up with a rope a bag containing my heavy camera equipment.

What followed was a cold, cramped, snowy vigil. Not a deer moved anywhere within sight. Just before noon, I replaced the camera in its bag, lowered it, and dropped the rope end. That soft sound is probably what made a doe, standing hidden nearby, stamp her foot. I froze in place. Minutes later the female, followed by two bucks, walked directly below me. The bucks sparred briefly, cracking antlers together, then one sniffed at my camera bag, made a hoof scrape right next to it, and finally all three walked away. After climbing down, so did I, feeling defeated.

WINTER

Everywhere the rut, that most active, most dramatic season of the whitetailed deer, is followed by winter, the most severe annual test for the survival of the species. Those whitetails that have escaped the legal hunting seasons (and poaching as well) intact and have lived through the rut must now survive several months of the "hunger moon," the most grim season, the time when food is least abundant and least nutritious throughout deer habitat from the Mexican border northward as far as deer range. If survival is not actually more difficult in the northern half of this range, it certainly seems to be.

From spring through the autumn rut whitetail herds roam widely, fattening on immense varieties of plant foods found on dry (oak, hickory, and beech) hardwood ridges, along the edges of swamps, and in farmers' cropfields. Nutrition is good and the living is comparatively easy. It's warm, or warm enough, and in some states during mid-summer, too hot. But from Maine and Nova Scotia westward to Montana, December begins the most desperate battle of all to survive in the wintering areas—or "yards"—at least until April. Yards in the North are somewhat sheltered woodland areas where deer congregate and concentrate during the depth of winter.

Rutting season on a snowy December morning in Iowa, on the edge of farmland. The deer turn suddenly toward the sound of the camera's motor drive. We were well hidden in a ground-level blind nearby.

In the wild world, such creatures as waterfowl, songbirds, and caribou escape winter by flying or migrating far away where living conditions will be better. Bears and ground squirrels hibernate, resting and sleeping through brutal winter, in comparative comfort underground. But deer have no options except to stay and tough it out wherever they always live.

Whitetails apparently can sense the coming of severe weather and, especially across the northern Midwest and all of Canada, they begin the trek to cedar swamps and other refuges of dense cover well before the worst storms strike. Once actually in a deer yard, the animals are reluctant to leave as long as any great snow depth covers the ground. The deeper the snow accumulations, the fewer deer wander out and away from the yards to forage. Although some may starve in time, the sedentary existence does not consume as much energy as searching for food far away.

For many years, biologists have closely studied and monitored northern deer in winter, and most agree that too many questions about deer behavior still remain. When there is about two feet or so in snow depth, individual stronger deer may continue to explore outward from a winter yard to feed on any browse they can reach. Beyond that depth, they will bed down and seemingly try to conserve what energy exists. When they do go foraging, they tend to follow existing deer trails rather than break new ground in the food search. During the most severe winters the toll is heavy, sometimes terrible. Winter-weakened and confined deer are the easiest prey of predators. Often a deep lethargy sets in. Malnutrition and parasites plus unknown other factors kill some older and younger animals.

In hilly regions, especially of the Northeast, whitetails tend to concentrate on south-facing slopes where on bright days the sun's greater intensity (than on flat lands) helps husband energy. Deer yards on such southern slopes are well known because deer return to them winter after winter. For many years, as many as seven hundred whitetails have been counted along one ridge in western New York less than three miles long and a half-mile in width. Similar yards exist in other northern states and provinces.

Beleaguered deer may try to keep trails open between yard bedding sites and certain kinds of logging or pulpwood operations that litter the ground with edible browse. Supplemental feeding by concerned humans of tree slashings and hay may also help bring some deer through a difficult winter, but there is great disagreement among biologists over the value of this. Some deer will eat hay (although not digest all kinds properly); others will not. Possibly this winter deer feeding may be of much greater benefit to the feeders than to the recipients.

The quality of hay fed to deer can make all the difference. Almost all deer can digest high-quality *alfalfa* hay, but cannot manage coarse, low-grade hay. In too many supplemental feeding programs, people often use lower quality hay or offer the hay too late, after the deer have begun to starve. At that point the rumen microbes in the deer's stomach have begun to die off, and thus the deer cannot digest anything. Such deer are often found dead around feeders, with their stomachs full of hay. This is what has led to the misconception that deer can't digest hay. Another problem is the feeding of corn in the winter. Deer can founder on corn, developing acidosis, and thus again be killed by human kindness.

Activity almost ceases in northern deer yards during high winds and plunging temperatures, or on warm days when the snow crust easily crumbles, and immediately after storms. Although deer of a group may bed down near one another, there is no evidence that any ever huddle near enough together to share body heat. When the mercury falls to 20 below or lower, deer must stand and exercise for periods to maintain circulation, increasing energy demands and the need for food.

During early mornings late in winter, after freezing and thawing has crusted the surface hard enough to support a deer, stronger animals may again wander about to browse on tree branches, which until then had been out of reach. But this supply is also quickly exhausted close to deer yards, as foliage is stripped and even the hemlock cuttings, done by porcupines, are quickly consumed.

If there is ever a time and place when the gentle brown-eyed Bambi myth is totally destroyed, it is in late winter in a northern whitetailed deer yard. The more the grip of winter tightens, the more viciously some deer fight for scarce food. The oldest animals and fawns feel the pinch first; not only are the latter unable to reach food, but they are bullied and kicked aside by larger deer. Males dominate females and females dominate fawns, including their own, just for tidbits they wouldn't touch at any other time. The survival instinct is much more powerful now than are family ties, as any strong deer now drives any weaker deer away with flailing hooves. If a fawn becomes too weak to follow its mother through deep snow, it will only be ignored.

Field studies in the northern Midwest and Canada have shown that severe winters can kill half of the fawn crop that had managed to live through the autumn. Those fawns that do survive may never grow as large or robust as they might have if food had been plentiful during their first winter. Severely weakened by malnutrition, some pregnant does are

The northern does of late autumn are fat and sleek, and the thickly matted hair is long, all in readiness for the bitter, grueling "hunger moon" ahead.
Overleaf: *Rattling antlers is a good way to attract curious bucks within camera range during the rut. The deer in this photo came to investigate the sound of our cracking antlers together from a blind.*

It is the rut in northern Minnesota, and a fine buck is approaching all the females he encounters, testing for signs of estrus. During this time, he does not waste much time or effort on anything else. **Right:** *A Missouri buck is sleek, fat, and ready for the winter ordeal, which will not be nearly as severe here as farther north in places like Minnesota, Quebec, and Ontario.*

known to reabsorb the embryos they carry and not give birth to new fawns in the spring. Resorption (rather than abortion) is the female whitetail's way of eliminating a dead fetus. During the worst winters in the past, as many as two million whitetails have perished continent-wide. Of course it doesn't happen overnight, but it does happen over many weeks in remote yards where few humans ever venture when the temperature hovers around zero and below.

An increasing number of deer biologists are convinced that extreme cold alone is not nearly the threat to deer in winter as is cold *plus* lack of adequate nutrition. The problem often is too many deer too quickly eating up the available food supply, so that all are undernourished. Much remains unknown about the carrying capacity of various deer range lands. More deer could be legally harvested—hunted—in most northern states if winter forage could be maintained at a higher level.

Once in the late 1960s I snowshoed around the edges of a Minnesota deer yard toward the tag end of winter. What I found was not a pretty sight. Everywhere was a sharp, definite browse line on trees as high as I could reach or a large deer on hind legs could crop the twigs and branches. Here two deer

were down, and a hundred yards farther were a dozen more that probably would never stand again. One stiff carcass was covered by snow and the skeleton of another, eaten by a bobcat, was all that remained. On the survivors, the skin hung loosely on the frames and bones were easily visible through the heavy winter coats. The same animals that would instantly gallop away in summertime when a man approached, now only stared at me through dull eyes.

But near one deer yard I also witnessed uncharacteristic behavior. A party of pulpwood cutters came to work nearby and began sawing down birch trees. As soon as some older, stronger deer heard the chainsaw, they hurried to the sound and stood within full view of the workers to eat the crowns of the toppled trees.

Strange as it may seem, deer in the southernmost United States also have winter survival problems. Even in Louisiana and subtropical Florida, there may be an annual deer loss that corresponds with the winter die-offs in the north. In swamp country, winter rain can raise water levels enough to isolate deer on a few ridges or islands of high ground, where all suitable food is quickly eaten. The rising water depth can be roughly

Often heavy rains falling in autumn on Louisiana bayou country suddenly raise water levels and cause whitetail deer to seek areas of higher ground and to concentrate there until rains end.

A buck moves through a central Manitoba thicket at the end of the rutting season and at the onset of winter. Already food is scarce.

compared to the increasing depth of snow in the north. During several critical winters, rising waters in Florida's Everglades and Big Cypress Swamp have cut the deer herd by as much as one-third. Malnutrition, parasite infestations, and pneumonia are what finally kill mostly the fawns, the oldest adults, and yearlings, in that order.

SPRING, SUMMER, AND FORAGING FOR THE RETURN OF FALL

Fortunately winters do not last forever. As early as March in the Southeast and late May in the North Woods, vegetation becomes luxuriant again. The last snow melts. Everywhere, new forbs and succulent growth, plus warmth and longer days, gradually restore the strength of deer herds. All whitetails shed their heavy winter coats for the new, lightweight red ones. Fawning time has come for the fittest does that have survived the winter. Any fetus that has also survived is likely to become a very durable fawn.

The whitetailed deer's gestation period is approximately seven months. So a fawn conceived during the rut of November will be "dropped" in late May or early June, by which time the health and vigor of the female should be fully restored. As birthing time approaches, a doe will leave her herd—usually her winter yardmates—and seek out some lonely place. Biolo-gists who have observed whitetails for a long time disagree as to whether the does prefer—or actually select—some special birthing places or whether it happens wherever the mother happens to be. I have found a number of fawns within a day or so after birth and they were in widely different kinds of places. The most attractive was in an open Minnesota woodland, beside a mossy deadfall where pink moccasin flowers grew. I found another fawn in a northern Michigan bog while trout fishing and this place was so infested with mosquitoes and black flies that it seemed the fawn couldn't possibly survive the onslaught. From this it seems the birth takes place wherever the doe happens to be.

If she is young, or if it is a first birth, the doe will probably bear a single fawn. An older mother in good condition might drop twins or even triplets. There is the extraordinary record of a Texas whitetailed doe that produced four sets of triplets—a dozen fawns—in the first five years of her life. Occasionally quadruplet fawns are born, but almost never do all four survive. In fact only rarely do all of the triplets reach maturity. One mystery is why better-fed does bear more females while undernourished does have more male fawns. But within a week or two of fawning, more female than male fawns are left alive and this ratio continues to widen as the young grow older. Female fawns also remain with or near their mothers much

The "hunger moon" has arrived. This doe was sitting in a snowstorm just outside my window in Montana. She did not move until she was almost covered up by the drifts and invisible.

longer: for up to two years after birth. Northern whitetail male fawns average about seven pounds at birth, females average about six pounds.

For a healthy doe, birth is quick and practically bloodless. Normally it takes only a few seconds from the time the fawn's head emerges until it is free on the ground. The umbilical cord breaks when the doe turns around to lick and nuzzle the fawn. The whole process has been very rarely seen in the wild, but in captivity the second of twin fawns is born about eight minutes after the first. The mother eats the placental sacs. The fawns struggle to stand on unsteady legs almost immediately.

Few animals are more appealing than the tawny red, newborn fawns with their large, fearful eyes, and irregular rows of white spots along the flanks and back. The hooves are yellowish at birth, but darken in a few minutes. For a day or so, the mother will stay beside or very near the newborns, which gain strength with amazing speed. Within an hour or less a fawn can nurse with the mother lying down, and soon after that can nurse while the doe is standing. In the beginning, the young whitetails nurse for a few minutes at a time and at two- to three-hour intervals, lying down to rest between feeding periods. As they grow older and stronger, some fawns tend to grow rough and impatient when nursing, but this usually results in a swift kick by the mother. The milk is much richer than that of a domestic milk cow, with several times the fat, solids, and protein content. Twin fawns normally nurse simultaneously.

After the first days, female whitetails spend only brief periods with fawns until the time the fawns are strong enough to travel and rejoin small herds (probably their original bands) of related females and young deer. Mothers travel during the day to feed on spring greens, returning at intervals to nurse the fawns. Meanwhile the fawns rest, gain weight, brush away bothersome bugs, anticipate the next meal, and "freeze" in case danger approaches or anything unnatural takes place. They do not move from where they are left by the mother. Flattened on the ground and motionless, the spotted coats are superb camouflage even in a green woods. Twin or triplet fawns are cached separately, seldom close together. They are left alone regardless of how foul and wet the weather becomes.

It is during this early period of frequent separations that mortality from predators (a list that includes pet dogs as well as bobcats, coyotes, lynxes, bears, and other wild hunters) is highest. This is also the time when the most fawns are picked up by well-meaning humans who believe the fawns are lost or abandoned. Such "rescue" is illegal almost everywhere, because whitetail mothers do not abandon healthy fawns and almost always are watching unseen, from not so far away.

In time—a few weeks—whitetail fawns are able to follow

Above: A Minnesota doe ventures cautiously into sunlight at the edge of a forest to feed in early morning in late springtime. She has a new fawn hiding not far away. **Right:** A Minnesota fawn just a few days old, probably belonging to the doe in the photo above, remains absolutely motionless despite the approach of a photographer. Fawns should never be forced to move, touched, picked up, or carried away—in any way "rescued."

their mothers everywhere and are gradually force-weaned to eat the same nutritious plants she eats, while learning to test the breezes all around for signs of trouble. Like most mammal mothers, does teach by example. Older, experienced mothers are likely to be the better teachers because their own survival skills are better honed. Just knowing when to stand motionless and watch, and when to run immediately from danger, can be the difference between life and death for the fawn. Summed up, the most resourceful, wary does have the best chance to raise resourceful, wary fawns to adulthood.

By contrast, male whitetails are aloof from fawn-rearing and other family responsibility. Summer is mostly an idyllic, vagabond time (or as close to idyllic as a prey species can know) of living off the bounty of the land, bachelor style. Bucks at least seem to be totally consumed with feeding and accumulating the body fat they will need later during the rut and to survive another winter.

It is believed that very small fawns have no detectable scent and cannot be smelled by predators, which has always been hard for me to believe. But one warm humid evening in southern Ohio, I did watch a large whitetailed buck in red summer coat and developing velvet antlers walk to within a few feet of where a fawn was hidden. If that buck detected the presence of the fawn, which may even have been its own, it showed no sign whatever. However, this odorless babyhood of fawns—this natural protection—does not last when tarsal glands begin to function. All deer from young to the largest males have the same instinctive urge to leave scent wherever they go.

Although the "hunger moon," the winter toll of deer both in the northern forests as well as in the southern United States, can be devastating, in west Texas and in the Southwest the most lethal season may be mid- to late-summer when drought and overgrazing by the domestic livestock that share the range combine to weaken or even eliminate deer in wholesale numbers. When these droughts occur, water sources quickly evapo-

Below: *Even when bedded down, whitetails are always on the alert, dozing only fitfully. This doe watches ahead while her ears are tuned in to anything taking place behind.* **Overleaf:** *This Minnesota fawn, two to three weeks old, is spending a warm summer day bedded among wildflowers until its mother returns to nurse it.*

Does with twin fawns usually do not leave the two as close together when going away to feed as these twins are here. Soon after this photo was taken, the mother returned to nurse the fawns.

Left: *This Montana fawn photographed in Glacier National Park is old and strong enough to begin moving about and following its mother on daily travels.* **Right:** *The northwestern Montana fawn is spending the first weeks of life in the lush growth and wildflowers of June.*

A nervous doe with a very young fawn is always alert for danger. In this photo, she stomps a foot to try to provoke some motion from the photographer, crouched in a portable blind. If the photographer had moved, the doe would have used the visual clues for identification.

rate, and the browse on which whitetails depend is eaten or dries up and blows away. During such summers, there are deer die-offs almost as severe and even more sudden than those during the worst of the northern winters. Not only do deer die when ranchlands are overgrazed and sere, but only a small percentage of does will bear fawns the following spring. Bucks may not develop the same handsome racks of antlers during droughts that they would normally attain by September or October.

With or without undue hardship, whitetails live fairly short lives. In captivity and with the best of nutrition, fifteen years is near the absolute maximum longevity, but purely wild whitetails rarely reach half that age. Wherever whitetailed deer populations are large and regular hunting seasons are held, few deer live beyond their fourth or fifth autumn. Besides the legal sport hunting harvest, disease, weather, predation, poaching, plus a heavy nationwide highway kill assure a short average lifespan.

Diet

Diet is an important factor in any whitetailed deer's longevity. Whitetails are browsers that seem to sample anything growing where they live. In spring and early summer they may sometimes graze on tender grasses, but greatly prefer to feed through second-growth woods and brushland, biting off tender twigs, leaves, and buds. Of course they utilize—concentrate on—certain foods first, as long as the supply lasts. The deer then resort to less favorite forbs, twigs, leaves, and buds when everything else is gone. The diet of whitetails across North America varies so much and includes so many items that just to catalogue the eight-hundred-plus known wild plants would require an entire volume.

This much is certain: An average whitetail requires about six pounds of browse—food—per day to survive in optimum health. The daily intake will average more during the abundance of summer, and much less during the winter. Once imitating a hungry deer for my own knowledge, I picked six pounds of typical browse with the fingers of one hand, trying to imitate a nibbling deer. It required about two hours, and I filled a bushel basket. Deer have incisor teeth only on the bottom of their mouths with no opposing teeth, so they literally tear off, rather than bite cleanly, any twigs or leaves, leaving fibrous strands behind.

In general order of preference, whitetails browse first on sprouts, then on seedlings of trees and shrubs, so-called weeds, flowering plants, and vines. Deer foods might be divided into three general categories: highly preferred, acceptable, and adequate or barely adequate. Where populations are low, the deer can concentrate on the most preferred, most nutritious vegetation, never destroying the stock that will regenerate. As numbers increase they depend more and more on just acceptable, moderately nutritious items. When they must rely too much on the least preferred foods, it is an indication of too many deer, or deteriorating habitat, or both. It should be noted here that the deer's preferred foods are also those that are best for its health, one important way in which deer differ from most humans.

Northern whitetails heavily utilize aspen, white cedar, yew, and ground hemlock. Regionally in the northern part of their range, blueberries and young maples are important. In their southern range, a list of staples would include greenbrier, flowering dogwood, black gum, maples, white oak, plum, sassafras, and sumac. The species will avidly consume and compete with other wildlife for the fallen acorns, rich in carbohydrates, from many kinds of oak trees. Buckbrush, bearberry, dogwood, chokecherry, and aspen are popular where whitetails have invaded the West. Everywhere the species will eat certain mushrooms, especially puffballs, and surprisingly, poison ivy. Strange as it may seem, whitetails have also been seen nibbling on carrion fish (because of mineral deficiency?), oranges, grapefruit, pears, on the carcass of a porcupine, and on their own fallen antlers.

All deer need to add some body fat before the onset of winter, and they do this by a process is known as lipogenesis. For reasons not entirely clear, there are huge acorn crops during some years and a great scarcity in other years. During abundant mast crops, a deer's body growth and fat accumulation is high. So is its health and survivability. The opposite is true during years when the acorn supply is low. Deer get fatter faster on acorns than on any other food, and they know the locations of all oak trees in their territories and beyond.

It is interesting that whitetails will consume foods with such mean sounding names as fleabane, greasewood, sourdock, sourwood, soapberry, stinkweed, skunkwood sumac, and skunk cabbage as well as plants with sweet sounding names such as honeysuckle, beautyberry, sweet William, sweetbay, wild strawberry, and wild rose. Many of these foods, sweet or sour, are eaten only at specific times when the ripeness or extent of growth exactly suits their taste.

Being cud-chewers or ruminants, deer are able to consume much food quickly in order to spend less time thus exposed and then to retreat to the safety of heavier cover. All newly eaten material is held in the first or upper stomach. Once the deer is bedded down after feeding, food or cud is rechewed before passing on into three more stomach compartments. As vegetarians, deer have no gall bladders but instead produce bile in the liver, which goes directly into the small intestine via the common bile duct.

Deer also will gorge on many nonwild foods or agricultural crops, not endearing them to many farmers. Amazingly, they are able to distinguish (and prefer to eat from) fertilized (with commercial nitrogen-phosphorus fertilizers) fields rather than from a nonfertilized area. Deer will invade apple orchards to browse the twigs and eat the fruit, quite often at night when it is safest. Few whitetails will ever pass up shelled ear corn, many garden vegetables, and high-quality (tender) domestic hay. Especially in winter, herds of deer will crowd around corn cribs and eat all they can reach. It is difficult in many parts of the Northeast and Midwest to raise a summer garden without fencing away the local deer.

If summer in North America has been typically warm, with adequate rainfall, and a good mast crop, whitetailed deer will begin golden autumn looking fat and sleek, their red coats exchanged for winter gray. Male antlers are almost fully grown. The fawns are large, agile, and now nearly as tough and athletic as their parents. A few of the more precocious, stronger female fawns will even breed this first fall when barely eight months old. Thus another cycle begins in the life of the whitetailed deer.

The more I observe and photograph whitetailed deer, the more I am amazed at what they can endure. I once saw a doe struck by a speeding car and tossed ten feet into the air, land almost upright, stagger off the road and then jump a barbed wire fence to disappear. My friend and New York State wildlife cameraman Charles Alsheimer photographed a six-point buck that had lost a front leg but otherwise was perfectly healthy and seemed able to keep up with other deer. He also focused on a doe that seemed to live normally despite dragging a compound-fractured hind leg behind. The species' ability to survive is simply phenomenal.

Left: *This doe is foraging along the edges of a pond in the Ozark foothills. Late summer and early autumn are times to feed heavily on the bounty of the season. During the upcoming rut, there will be less time for that.* **Right:** *In summer, deer browse frequently around the edges of lakes and ponds where fresh green vegetation may sprout before it does in dense woodlands. In some northern areas, the water is also a handy escape from hunting wolves.*

Right: *Toward the end of summer, whitetailed fawns and does regroup—reassemble—into small herds, as here in the Ozarks.* **Overleaf:** *In many areas of the Southeast, as here in northern Florida, whitetails live in and around the edges of cypress forests and swamps. Bucks fight and breed in this damp environment, and depend at times on aquatic vegetation for food. All whitetails can swim. Cypress swamps are fairly secure refuges, too.*

THE BEHAVIOR OF A WHITETAIL

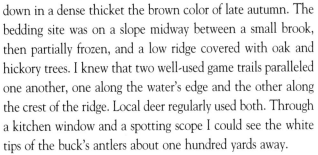

One cold morning in December, toward the end of Ohio's deer-hunting season, I watched a heavy old buck with splendid antlers bed down in a dense thicket the brown color of late autumn. The bedding site was on a slope midway between a small brook, then partially frozen, and a low ridge covered with oak and hickory trees. I knew that two well-used game trails paralleled one another, one along the water's edge and the other along the crest of the ridge. Local deer regularly used both. Through a kitchen window and a spotting scope I could see the white tips of the buck's antlers about one hundred yards away.

Not long after the whitetail bedded down, two hunters in red caps and coats appeared on the scene. After chatting and gesturing (planning strategy?) for a few moments where an iron bridge crossed the brook, they began to slowly hunt up-stream on the two almost parallel game trails. Warm, and with coffee brewing on the stove, I had a ringside seat for whatever happened next. One or both of the men would *have* to walk very close to a trophy buck and flush it. And then?

Cautiously the two moved ahead, stopping at intervals to study the terrain all around them. They seemed to be experienced stalkers. I *knew* that the deer would at any moment bounce suddenly out of its bed and give somebody a running shot. One hunter paused to look around when barely forty feet from the buck, did not spot it, and continued on unaware. (Later on I paced off the distance.) I could still see the antler tips when the hunters disappeared from view.

Why did that animal choose to hide when it could so easily have run—or sneaked—away when the hunters were still far out of gun range? A light wind was blowing from the men generally toward the buck, and the deer must have smelled them. It must also have heard them talking. We know that a deer's brain is small and reasoning is impossible. The only logical explanation is that some survival instinct we cannot understand dictated that it was safer in this situation to play 'possum than to run. The truth is that, despite all their keen senses and speed afoot, older male deer, especially, often prefer to hide rather than run in times of danger. It is certainly a "trick" they often use to avoid humans, as many students of whitetails have noted. It may also be a means at other times to escape wild predators.

FROM PLAY TO AGGRESSION

Deer behavior may seem strange and unfathomable to people. But all of it has to do with survival, with living in whatever the environment, with avoiding all kinds of predators, coping with parasites, people, and weather. During the summer when forage is abundant in North America, healthy whitetails of all ages engage in behavior we might call "play," but which is really something else. This begins among fawns as soon as they are old enough to come out of hiding and are able to run at high speed. Assembled in a small herd, the fawns chase and jump over one another, wheel, dodge, butt heads, and gambol not unlike children racing around a playground. But this be-havior isn't limited to the youngest. I have seen yearlings and even mothers occasionally join in the cavorting, and there are two possible explanations for this behavior.

Very early in the rutting season, when they meet, bucks test one another with body language and by brushing antlers. Very soon even brothers that may have spent the summer together in peaceful bachelorhood will become serious rivals for available females.

A small Iowa buck slashes out with hooves at a doe in what seems to be a dispute over food or space.

To monopolize a food source, to establish dominance in a female herd, or both, does can be very aggressive, often lashing out at their "friends," even at their own fawns, with forefeet. Bambis they're not.

Some scientists now regard deer (and other animal) "play" as an index of environmental conditions. Whitetails living in a richer environment, with food aplenty, play more often and more vigorously than those in a depleted habitat. For comparison, healthy human children play harder and longer than undernourished children, who are listless. At least more deer play seems to take place where the population density is low and the quality of the habitat is high. During years when natural deer foods are scarce, or when whitetails fill their range to absolute capacity, they must spend more time foraging and have less time left to play. So playing may well be evidence that all is well with a local deer herd. I hope so, because I often watch them playing—running and jumping exuberantly—in my back pasture.

However, there is another and maybe a better reason for deer play, at least for fawn play. It is training and conditioning for the hard life ahead, for long-term survival. Running and jumping build stronger muscles and develop lung capacity, increasing endurance. The same awkward maneuvers a fawn uses in apparent play can later help it escape from predators. It can help make the fawn more sure-footed. Older bucks play the least, and some not at all.

One mysterious aspect of whitetail play that I have noticed is that it usually starts and stops suddenly, as if on some silent signal. One biologist explained that this is a vigilance measure; a deer can better detect approaching danger by stopping abruptly and then standing to listen. It is like being able to hear a faint sound, only after all other noise stops.

I do not believe that whitetail play ever intends injury or is the result of aggression, as is sometimes the case with other species. This is not to say that whitetailed deer are meek and mild. In fact they can be highly aggressive among themselves and will fight viciously in other situations. Not only will they fight for food in winter and for sexual partners in autumn, but they will also compete for living space and for status. One biologist reported does fighting for what he believed to be the best fawning sites. However, the most intense competition is usually over a limited or diminishing food supply. The most clearcut aggression among does I have ever seen has been on some Texas ranches, around the feeders that automatically dispense shelled corn in limited amounts. Strong, determined deer usually monopolize the free grain.

Even when food is readily available, a deer's social rank in its herd or group must eventually be established. If bluffing and posturing fail to work as they normally do, a physical confrontation is the only way to settle it. Most showdowns probably take place when unfamiliar animals meet or are mixed, as following the hectic population reshuffling right after an open hunting season. In established herds, social rank is determined early, maybe during the play periods of fawns. Following a two-year study of whitetailed deer in San Patricio County, Texas, biologist Ed Michael concluded that a certain amount of aggression may even be necessary to maintain the species' high reproductive rate.

During recent decades, scientists, using controlled conditions, have studied the effects of crowding on everything from Norway rats and white laboratory mice to parrots, wild rabbits, prairie dogs, and deer, and the conclusions are always the same. When only a pair or a few of a species are living in or are confined to a suitable habitat, they prosper and get along very well. But the more the numbers increase within the same habitat, the more frequent and more violent the conflict that takes place. Normal social behavior changes to abnormal behavior, aggression, and savagery. Health deteriorates. Therefore much fighting outside the breeding season may also indicate an overpopulation of deer. From the animal studies, we might also conclude that human overcrowding and overpopulation of the earth are responsible for the strife, turmoil, wars—the social and health problems that threaten our own survival today.

THE MOON, THE RAIN, AND THE WIND

American Indians of earlier times believed that both the weather and moon phase affected deer behavior, and many modern observers do not disagree. Over a period of years on a Georgia hunting preserve, manager Dave Morris kept detailed records of deer movement and behavior. He found the animals to be stimulated and to circulate more on days when the temperature was normal or below normal. On days with an above-average reading, whitetails were sluggish and most of their movement was concentrated in the mornings.

With an eye both on the barometer and deer activity, Morris noted that the Georgia whitetails in his study area were much more active when the barometric pressure was above 29.00 inches. Also there was more movement when the humidity was low, and noticeably less movement during periods of haze, fog, and rain (all high humidity symptoms), when the deer became extremely secretive.

So in Georgia at least, and possibly elsewhere, whitetails are most active of all when the barometer is high, but the temperature and humidity are low. Feeding tends to be most furious and activity tends to quicken just before the arrival of a storm front. As many skilled woodsmen and -women have long contended, deer as well as other animals seem uncanny

Top: *A buck's antler is solid bone, hardened and difficult to snap, but one whole antler of this male was broken off during a fight.* **Right and above:** *The bucks in the photo at right were just testing one another tentatively, early in the rut. In the photo above, rivals of equal size and strength were having at one another with no holds barred. The two began fighting suddenly while we were photographing a third buck from our ground-level blind in Texas.*

in their ability to anticipate a sharply rising or falling barometer. In fact some old-timers predict weather on the basis of deer activity they see.

Observations on the moon's influence on deer, if any, are harder to find and document than the effect of the barometer. It's much more difficult to observe animals at night, even in moonlight, and the laws in many states today do not encourage people to wander around a deer woods after dark, the period when deer poachers do most of their killing. But deer are probably able to see as well, or almost as well, during the dark of the moon as during a full phase. So can most deer predators. Deer do not sleep soundly for long periods as do healthy humans, but instead rest always on the alert.

The plain truth, summed up, is that neither biologists nor experienced outdoorspeople fully understand the relationship between animal behavior, barometric pressure, and weather. But it can be said that deer and other wild creatures are sensitive to barometric changes, even to moon phases, in ways that humans have long ago lost, or cannot possibly understand.

For a number of reasons deer, like most hooved animals, usually move facing into the wind when feeding. This way, the scent of any predator ahead will be carried to sensitive noses. At the same time the feeding deer is also moving farther and farther away from a predator that might be stalking from behind, who is also using the wind to detect its prey. But this feeding-while-constantly-moving behavior has another purpose as well: It helps to prevent overbrowsing of vegetation in any one area. At the same time, nibbling the tips of some plants is actually pruning that helps to stimulate growth.

DOES A WHITETAIL USE BODY LANGUAGE?

Everywhere and almost anytime within any range in North America, the whitetail's behavior is shaped by predators and predation. That means always, absolutely always being alert. In wilder portions of the range, such traditional natural predators as wolves, cougars, coyotes, and lynx, plus humans, are the hunters to watch out for. But even in areas where all natural, large predators were long ago eliminated, deer have no chances for relaxation. In these areas, far too often domestic dogs running wild have more than replaced the cougars and the wolves. The toll taken by dogs out of control on the fringes of some urban areas is excessive and deplorable.

Increased deer movement seems to occur just ahead of an advancing storm front, especially late in the year. But most of the animals lie low, or move very little during the peaks of storms.

Watching whitetails for many years during all seasons through the viewfinder of a camera has revealed many behavioral traits to me. When a deer is feeding with its head down, and the tail flicks quickly, sometimes almost imperceptibly from side to side, it is a signal that the deer is about to raise its head. The reason may be only innate caution, but it might also be that constant fear of a predator somewhere on the horizon. I once watched a doe become increasingly nervous this way, long before a pair of boxer dogs—house pets running loose—came into view. The doe easily managed to give these two the slip. But just before bolting, I saw the deer raise her tail to the horizontal, a tell-tale sign of immediate departure.

Another sign of fear, agitation, or readiness to flush is when an animal holds its head low and licks the sides of its mouth. On the other hand, holding the head high and curling back the upper lip, ears back or to the side, is a sign the deer likes or relishes something. This lip-curling by a buck, called flehmen, is most often seen during the rut when the animal detects and savors the scent of females coming into estrus. I've found that any buck thus soaking up sensory information is usually an easier one to approach and photograph. (Incidentally, I've almost never seen a doe perform this lip-curling behavior.)

Whitetailed deer exhibit body language that is even easier to interpret than that of humans. Late in November I watched a Montana buck feeding, listlessly because it was the rut, when suddenly it raised its head high, swollen neck extended, and held its tail straight back. A few moments later, I saw the reason for the change in attitude. Another buck was advancing, this one with its ears laid back and the hair atop its neck and shoulders erected. What followed was a brief, nonviolent use of body language to establish dominance in the area of Deep Creek.

The first buck, which carried the heavier antlers and larger body, emphasized those assets by walking forward, toward the invader, on stiff legs. The newcomer tried more threatening body language to compensate for its smaller size, but it didn't work. Number two stopped its advance just short of touching antlers, turned away, and disappeared into a stand of juniper trees.

The body language most often seen and the least subtle, is flagging or tail waving. Mostly it means the animal is alarmed or uneasy. Does wave or raise tails when feeding to keep other deer from crowding too close. If accompanied by foot stomping and staring, the deer, either buck or doe, is trying to get some object it cannot clearly identify to move and reveal itself. When feeding some distance from her fawn, a doe flags—an easy means to keep in touch with the fawn. More nervous flagging might tell fawns to either come closer or get ready to run.

OLDER—AND WISER?

Biologists differ, often radically, over whether a deer's behavior changes very much as it grows older. Studies seem to indicate both yes and no. Again from the viewpoint of a serious, professional wildlife photographer, it seems to me that they do definitely change with age, especially in areas where there is heavy hunting pressure from humans. It is possible, for example, to drive down country roads all across North America, just before dusk, and spot small bands of deer standing tentatively, or feeding, around forest edges. But after autumn leaves fall and the first salvos of a new hunting season are heard, you can drive those same backroads and the land is empty of whitetails. Suddenly they go into hiding.

I am convinced whitetails do become "smarter," or at least shyer and more reclusive, the more hunting seasons and winters they survive. Male deer certainly grow more secretive as they mature. The oldest and biggest seem to vanish altogether. I knew at least two places in Texas where several super-trophy bucks lived, but the only signs of them were the great heart-shaped hoof prints left behind near muddy water tanks. No one ever saw them. But how am I certain that the age and size of the bucks matched the footprints? By picking up the discarded antlers of one and the whole skulls of two with interlocked antlers when spring arrived.

By thoroughly examining one such skull, I discovered that the animal was exactly 6½ years old when it died; biologists (or anyone, really) can determine the age of any deer from the development and condition of its teeth. I also measured the antlers of one buck, which I had never seen alive, and found them big enough to qualify for the Boone & Crockett Records of North American Big Game. (More about this in the antler chapter.)

For several falls I hunted deer in an Ohio township where the whitetail bucks never seemed to reach a ripe old age. At least no really big ones were ever shot by hunters. And none of the farmers I knew ever reported seeing any—until late in November when one of the biggest males in the entire state was killed on a highway by a beer truck. Two days later another even heavier buck was struck after dark by a motorist in a pickup. Both of these animals had managed to live so secretly in a typical agricultural community for six years, the last two or three with the kind of bragging-sized antlers that hunters covet, without being discovered!

One point raises another. Why were these two bucks killed at almost the same time on the same road? Why are there certain specific periods when the highway toll is heavy and other times when it is nearly nonexistent?

In the past (and to some extent today) salt and other chemicals have been used to melt snow on highways, and these unnatural salt "licks" have attracted deer to roadsides following storms. Blinded by oncoming headlights, the deer bolt and are struck. In scattered localities where old oak trees grow along highways, deer are attracted by the seasonal bonanza of fallen acorns—and pay for it. But the two Ohio bucks mentioned above were out and running during the rut, the single season everywhere in North America when the road kill is highest. In several states (New York, Pennsylvania, Ohio, Wisconsin, and Michigan among them) the highway death toll of whitetails at times has amounted to almost half the legal harvest of hunters.

One October night in 1987, a buck with antlers larger than any of the thousands taken during Michigan's hunting season was killed by a car in Washtenaw County. The driver said the huge animal "seemed to drop from the sky." So the same product of fifteen million years of evolution and trial has not yet learned to cope with high-speed thoroughfares and modern motor cars.

During the late fall rutting season of 1981, my friend Ken Wolfe, with special permission from Montana's state fish and game department, collected five tons of whitetail venison—seventy-five road kills—from just one twenty-mile stretch of Route 83 in the western part of the state! That was a little larger "harvest" than usual. On one November day alone, seven deer were struck by vehicles on this highway, which is heavily used by logging trucks, in one fifteen-minute period. Wolfe makes good use of the annual windfall: He is a wildlife rehabilitator and the meat comes in handy to feed the numerous injured hawks, eagles, and other raptors in his care.

DISEASES AND PARASITES THAT AFFECT DEER

The behavior, as well as the health and longevity of whitetails, is often affected by factors much smaller than cars. Parasites, for example. In the past, tularemia—a bacteria-caused disease that can be transmitted to humans and other animals by insects—has wiped out local populations of rabbits, and botulism has killed vast rafts of ducks, but to date deer have not been subject to such widespread plagues. But they have suffered from such destructive domestic livestock diseases as Bang's, hoof-and-mouth, necrotic stomatitis (a severe inflam-

mation of the mouth), tuberculosis, and other afflictions. Farmers consider hoof-and-mouth, a viral disease, the worst because it can spread from cattle to deer and back again. Fortunately, it is not fatal and outbreaks recently have been rare. There have been outbreaks of anthrax and blue tongue in Texas deer herds. A few whitetails have had rabies, probably after a bite from an infected dog or fox. Any rabid buck is one to be avoided because it will charge anything alive in its path.

Northern deer from time to time have been infested with larval lungworms and tapeworms. If otherwise healthy and well nourished, whitetails can withstand massive infestations of the lungworms. But the tapeworms can be more debilitating and are often a sign of overcrowding and resultant undernourishment. Deer pick up the tapeworms when they are forced by browse shortages to graze in cow pastures. During the late 1950s, a mysterious die-off in late summer struck in several eastern and southern states, and biologists are still baffled by it. Similar to a disease called "black tongue," this disease caused internal hemorrhaging and abnormally unwary behavior in the deer. Ticks are at least a small nuisance to whitetails in every section of their range.

Periodically, flies have been among the deadliest of enemies. Bot flies enter and hatch in deer nasal passages and throats, sometimes causing enough irritation and even brain damage to cause the animals to stop feeding. Warble flies penetrate beneath the hides of deer. Black flies and mosquitoes can make a northern whitetail or a southern coastal deer so miserable that it loses natural caution for predators in the single-minded attempt to escape the biting. On the other hand, I have seen Michigan deer endure clouds of mosquitoes that would have driven me crazy without the repellent smeared on all of my exposed skin. Mosquitoes concentrate around eyes, ears, nose, and lips; the last two can be cleared by licking.

DO HUMANS AFFECT THE WHITETAIL'S BEHAVIOR?

One question that must concern outdoorspeople everywhere is the effect of hunting on native whitetailed deer. It is easy to find many "logical" views both for and against hunting. But we cannot deny that America grew up eating whitetail venison and wearing buckskin. And in countless ways we are still people of the deer, especially in October and November when traditional hunting seasons begin.

As I write this in 1993, the continental population of deer is high, perhaps even higher in some areas than is best for the species. The actual scientifically managed harvest (the open hunting season) of deer every fall is a necessity to protect the environment from damage caused by overpopulation and that can be immense. So *not* to shoot deer during times when populations are high is really killing them with kindness. Allowing whitetailed deer to multiply regardless of the consequences is destructive to our land as well as an immense waste of meat more nutritious (and free of steroids and other chemicals) than domestic livestock.

Whitetailed deer are spectacularly productive, able to withstand a considerable hunting harvest plus road kill, and here is an excellent example. During the 1960s two bucks and four does were once enclosed inside the deer-proof George Reserve near Ann Arbor, Michigan. The enclosure was less than two square miles in size. Whitetails could neither escape nor enter from outside. The habitat was typical midwestern brush, marsh, woods, and grassy openings in what game managers described as "normal range." In a census five years later, refuge managers found an astonishing 220 deer inside the fence: thirty-six whitetails for every one of the original six in only a half a decade. But the once "normal range" was in a badly overbrowsed and terribly depleted condition. Starvation was the prospect for most of that deer herd, and very soon.

There may be reason to question some modern deer-hunting regulations and a philosophy of hunting that is still prevalent today. I'm speaking here of bucks-only hunting; of shooting only males, and with greatest emphasis on shooting the biggest males of all, the trophies. There remains great sentiment almost everywhere for the "does ain't deer" theory, that we should never kill them.

Understandably, most hunters enjoy the bigger challenge of pursuing the big bucks. And shooting only bucks, even during the rutting season, will not cause a herd to be less productive. One way or another, all mature does will be bred before the breeding season ends. But the constant drain on the supply of the biggest bucks might well have a detrimental effect in the long run. The more the strongest, largest males are shot, the more the breeding will be done by inferior animals. The result could be a deer herd too large, with an ever-increasing doe-to-buck ratio, with fewer genuine "trophy" bucks. In other words, it seems to be a matter of quantity versus quality. All deer biologists do not agree on that. But almost everywhere in the whitetail's range, biologists concur, there is every reason to harvest does in greater numbers, despite any aversion to it.

Now for an interesting and startling statistic. Each year about two hundred people perish in encounters or confrontations with wild creatures in the United States. Very seldom are the killers grizzly bears, mountain lions, orcas, sharks,

This buck is displaying lip-curl behavior, or flehmen. They do this after smelling the urine or bedding sites of does during the breeding season. The exact function of this is not known, but it is a widespread phenomenon in ungulates and probably facilitates scent-taste testing for signs of breeding readiness.

wolves, coral- or rattlesnakes, as one might expect. Instead at least two-thirds of all of the "killers" (an average 130 to 135 per year) are deer. (Bees are next most dangerous, with forty-three.) Many of the deaths come from vehicle collisions, especially at night, and from hunting accidents. But the number from deer attacks continues to creep upward. Some examples: A Colorado boy was killed by a deer he tried to free from entanglement in a fence. In Pennsylvania, a rutting buck attacked and gravely injured Bruce Gibbons and his thirteen-year-old son. A few days later in Alabama a farmer was found dead from multiple antler punctures. A Wisconsin archer was nearly killed by a wounded deer he was trailing. For no apparent reason, a buck attacked a sixty-nine-year-old lady who had paused at a rest stop near Lampasas, Texas. The most dangerous deer of all are those, especially males, that in one way or another have become used to people and are no longer afraid of them. This knowledge, that deer are the most dangerous critters in America, should be an integral part of popular deer lore.

Today's whitetail is certainly one of a kind. Originally a wilderness species, it today thrives in what might be called small game habitats close to civilization. No other large mammal in North America is equipped to do this. No other large species is so amenable to scientific management. To the sportsmen and -women in many states and provinces, *Odocoileus virginianus* is *the* big game animal—the only big game hunting possible. To many camera hunters and nonhunters it is the most attractive, most available large animal they are ever likely to see at close range.

Above: *A buck bites at its flank to dislodge a troublesome tick or other parasite.* **Right:** *An early winter snowstorm has passed, and does move out in the open to feed. As temperatures fall, activity decreases in deer herds.*

ANTLERS

Deer antlers seem to hold an extraordinary attraction for people, especially for hunters, but for scientists as well. Go anywhere in the world and you will soon find antlers or mounted heads tacked up on every kind of dwelling from sod huts, log cabins, and yurts, and to dens of modern American ranch homes and castles on the Rhine.

Of all deer antlers, those of whitetails are among the most elegant. Not the largest, certainly, but the most coveted. Men have spent vast sums of money and untold valuable time, have started fist fights, divorced wives, broken game laws, and vacated sanity just to obtain the trophy rack of a whitetailed deer to hang proudly in a club or office. In many communities, the stature or the best measure of a person is the size of the deer heads on his walls.

I am also well acquainted with two photographers who spend a (probably) unjustified amount of time every fall in the serious pursuit of trophy whitetail antlers . . . on film. The pictures in this book reveal that the Bauers are sometimes successful.

Throughout the ages, antlers and their velvet coverings have been (and still are in Asia) believed to cure everything from gout, anemia, and deafness, to impotency and lost desire. The fact that the substance never has relieved any of these, except perhaps psychologically, makes no difference. Deer antlers simply *look* virile, restorative, and so they must be. Compared to those of larger deer, especially elk, whitetail antlers traditionally have been of little value on the medicine market. The value for prestige purposes is another matter.

HOW DO WHITETAILS GROW ANTLERS?

Although we now know much about antlers and antler growth, some misconceptions remain. For example, animal horns and antlers are not the same. Such mammals as bison, bighorned sheep, gazelles, antelope, and many more have horns. Horns are made of keratin with a bony core and are retained as long as the animal lives. (Keratin is the same dead—without blood supply—protein substance of which hooves, hair, claws, and nails are composed.) The North American pronghorn (also called an antelope) is an exception; its horns have characteristic bony cores with outer horn sheaths, which are shed annually. Both males and female pronghorns have horns, although males horns are usually larger.

Antler, on the other hand, is wholly bone. Not only is it bone, but it is the fastest bone growth known. Only members of the deer family, Cervidae, grow antlers. Except for caribou and reindeer, only male deer have antlers, and these are shed and replaced every year. Very rarely a female whitetailed deer with a hormonal imbalance will grow small antlers. Whitetail bucks are programmed to develop antlers even before they are born. Pedicels—tiny antler bases—begin to develop on the tiny skull while the buck is still warm in its mother's womb.

Pedicels, or antler buds, which first appear as cowlicks in the hair of young fawns, are unique because they are living tissue links between the animal's skull and its antlers. The pedicels hold antlers in place for a while, even after the antlers die. Male fawns that are born later than normal in the

This is a buck with nontypical antlers of unusual mass. He may have experienced an injury early in his antler development. He grew up in Missouri farm country; many deer with unusually large racks are produced in this state.

summer, are undernourished early in life, are unduly stressed, or are deficient in testosterone development grow very small, or smaller than average, pedicels. That is extremely important because eventual antler size depends largely on the size of the pedicels. Bigger antler buds allow larger antlers with more points to develop. Good nutrition in early life is most important. Researchers agree that the size of a deer rack depends on age, nutritional history, and inherited traits, but they disagree greatly on the relative importance of these three factors.

A healthy whitetail buck begins to grow a new set of antlers in early spring, usually well before the year's fawns are born. The growth is triggered by light, or more specifically by the increasing daylight hours of springtime. From the instant new antlers emerge from the pedicels, they are covered with a network of blood vessels and nerve endings known as "velvet," because it looks and feels like light reddish-brown velvet or suede. This is the only regenerating skin found in mammals. The rapidly growing antlers receive blood both through the cores and from that outer velvety skin. How fast the antlers grow depends on heredity and nutrition.

If whitetail bucks get along very well with other deer during the summer, or avoid them altogether, it may be because antlers in the velvet are very fragile or tender. The velvet bruises easily, bleeds if punctured, and even suffers frostbite if retained on the antlers too late in the season. So a buck must remain fairly docile for a while to protect the crowning glory that will come later. If an antler in the velvet is seriously injured, not only will it be deformed in that injured place, but it may "remember" that injury and every succeeding annual rack will be similarly deformed as long as the buck lives. But as soon as the velvet is gone, the male whitetail undergoes a distinct personality change, from passive to active.

The whitetail antler-growing season across North America runs from March or April through September. Researcher Robert Brown of the Caesar Kleberg Wildlife Research Institute, Kingsville, Texas, learned that a deer's ribs become brittle and can break easily throughout the docile antler-growing period. The animal must borrow calcium and other minerals from its ribs and sternum to supply the growing antlers. Healthy bucks take this in stride; even if a bone is broken, it usually heals smoothly. Other deer researchers compare the stress of bone growth in one set of antlers to the growth of a fetus in a female.

The velvet-encased antlers on this young Wisconsin buck are only a few weeks old. Nutrition and heredity are factors that determine how large the antlers will eventually grow.

75

This Wisconsin buck was photographed in mid-June. With at least two months more in which to grow, this promised to be a magnificent trophy buck by the time the velvet peeled away in September.

It is interesting to note here that the study of the whitetail's amazing ability to mobilize minerals from skeletal bones to another part of the body, the antlers, may in time prove very helpful to solving the mysteries of osteosarcoma (bone cancer), and especially osteoporosis, a serious bone disease of older (mainly) Caucasian women.

Throughout the summer, except for the velvet antlers, whitetail bucks look and move about almost doelike. The necks are thin, and the wildness so noticeable in the eyes during the rut is missing. When there is disagreement, bucks respond like females, by rearing on hind legs and flailing with forefeet at an adversary's head. Anthony Bubenik of Guelph University, Ontario, believes that these summer bouts, rather than any later on, are what establish dominance in a herd. The later antler fights, he believes, are more for ritual or verification of ranking.

Sometime in October at the latest, the light alone, this time of waning light of fall, ends the annual cycle of antler growth. The hormone balance in every buck's body changes and the blood supply to the antlers is cut off. No longer nourished, the velvet dies and begins to peel away from antlers that are now mineralized and hardened. This is the time when an observant hiker in the woods will notice bucks with shreds of dark red or blackened velvet hanging from their heads. For

a while, blood may still ooze from around the pedicels and the bases of the antlers will be stained red. The velvet usually falls from largest males first and youngest ones last.

We have seen whitetail antlers of every color from polished ivory to dark mahogany or olive brown near the bases. The coloration comes from stain, from tannin in trees and leaves and from rubbing the antlers on bark, or from the stain of blood hemoglobin in the velvet. By the time the rut ends, much of the stain is either bleached or washed away by sunlight and rain. In my experience, the older, larger bucks are likely to hold the darkest stained antlers longest.

By late January, occasionally as late as February, most bucks have discarded their antlers. Antlers separate or are jarred free from the skull at the pedicel in a cold and bleak winter woods. These attachment spots soon heal, and a month or so later the first growth of new antlers is noticeable.

Cast (or shed) antlers do not forever litter the forest floor. They whiten and are soon used—recycled—by the myriad of small rodents and other animals that share a whitetailed deer's range. Eventually the antler minerals go back into the soil for utilization by other generations of wildlife.

THE NECESSITY OF ANTLERS

One mystery that remains, or at least is debated in scientific

This south Texas male is a typical, heavy, symmetrical, handsome ten-pointer in obvious good health. A specimen like this one makes the brittle brush country where it lives come alive.

It is difficult—no, impossible—to say what circumstances caused the strange, uneven antler formation in this south Texas buck.

The very high, narrow antlers of this Texas buck are common and widespread in one section of the Hill Country in that state.

conferences as well as in hunting camps, is why deer need antlers at all. Of what use is a whitetail buck's rack? Do they need the adornment at all in a society that some biologists debate is matriarchal?

Certainly during the summer season, does are the dominant sex. Individual does become more aggressive and ascendant with age. Females, not bucks, are usually the ones that make a habit of boldly raiding suburban orchards and vegetable and flower gardens. Old does also are the tyrants of snowy deer yards during the hunger moon. There is a good body of evidence that bucks live in summertime bachelor groups mostly because does shun them into the segregation. Even during the rut, some observers have noted, older irritable does drive much larger, persistent bucks away until *they* are ready to breed.

The most common if not always totally accepted theory is that bucks need antlers to clearly determine their place, their ranking in the local whitetail hierarchy. The biggest, healthiest bucks usually (but not absolutely always) have the heaviest antlers and do most of the breeding. In fact, as noted earlier, deer with very impressive racks may not even have to engage in any combat at all to succeed during the rut.

A theory more popular among laypeople than among scientists is that bucks grow antlers to defend against natural enemies. But if true, why don't female whitetails have them as well? And why don't males retain antlers longer, in fact throughout the winter season when predation is the worst? Even with the hardened, sharp-pointed antlers of fall, bucks under attack use their great speed and agility to escape rather than stand and resist. The only deer I ever saw thus in danger, from a pack of wild-running dogs in Maryland, kicked and slashed with front hooves rather than use its antlers. It managed to hold them off in that way until I could come to its rescue with a shotgun. So defense may be only a secondary use at best for antlers.

Several biologists and other keen observers of deer have another intriguing theory about the reason for antlers' presence. This might be mostly as attractors for females very much as the stunning colors of some male birds make them more desirable to the females. We have already noted how bucks with the most massive antlers manage most of the breeding, and although the theory is not absolute, it is possible that the sight of a heavy rack also subtly attracts does to the vicinity of the buck wearing it. Just as, one biologist noted, young women gravitate more toward men with sleek sports cars than to drivers of jalopies.

Evidence is even stronger that by the end of summer and of the antler-growing season, bucks may identify one another as much and as quickly by antlers as by scent, thereby eliminating the need to test one another each time they meet. At least in the semicaptivity of deer research stations where they can be monitored, bucks fight until one emerges the clear winner. After that, there is no more fighting between the two, which easily recognize one another until old age or illness changes the balance of strength or appearance.

In one experiment the antlers of a winner buck were partially sawed off. Perhaps because its rival was suddenly unrecognizable, the former loser immediately challenged it and won. So it is likely that once dominance is established in a whitetail herd or in an area, every resident buck will know its place just by a glance at antlers.

ANTLERS FOR WHITETAIL ADMIRERS

While scientists might be more interested in antler make-up and use, antler size and conformation are far more important to many whitetail admirers than how the antlers got that way. The conformation is hereditary. In their fine book, *Producing Quality Whitetails*, Texas biologists Murphy Ray and Al Brothers write that not only is the basic conformation inherited, but so are such oddities as drop tines, forked brow tines, forked main points, and roughness at the base. However, many of these characteristics may not become evident until the deer's third or fourth set of antlers is grown.

When living in average to good range, with adequate nutrition, whitetail bucks grow rapidly until almost two years old. After that, growth slows and has almost stopped after the animals reach four years of age, but the actual age when growth ends varies regionally. Initially, early growth goes into firm body-building rather than into antlers, which are small. But during its second or third summers, more and more of the deer's nutrition is channeled into growing larger antlers. On this schedule, each successive set of antlers is increasingly large until the animal is five and one-half or six and one-half years old. In other words, this is when the buck is usually in its prime, when, in my opinion, no other big game animal in America is so handsome, or so striking. If the buck survives longer than that, the size of its rack will gradually decrease with each passing year.

Whatever the conformation of a particular buck's antlers

Right: *At one and one-half years of age, during its second fall, this Montana buck has only one spike antler and probably will never grow a really handsome rack.* **Overleaf:** *Shorter antlers with heavy beams like this are common to bucks in Arkansas and Missouri farm country and in the Mississippi River bottoms.*

at three and one-half years of age, that same (or very similar) shape will never change, except to increase and then decrease in dimensions over the years. For this reason it is possible for a keen observer to recognize a certain buck in a forest from one autumn until the next. No two sets of antlers are ever exactly alike. I have "known" and renewed old acquaintances through my camera's viewfinder with several trophy whitetails for most of their lives. It is unfortunate that they didn't know and trust Peggy and me as well, or at least not well enough to let us approach closer for better photographs.

Deer of different localities and subspecies tend to have different or distinctive antler conformations, again reflecting heredity. But game biologists usually separate racks into three categories of conformation types, all very descriptive: "wide horn," "high horn," and "basket horn." The accompanying photos show these three shapes.

In addition, there are the nontypical or malformed antlers. A perfect typical rack would be a wide, high, or basket type, which is symmetrically shaped, the numbers and lengths of the tines or points being the same on each side. Nontypicals are asymmetrical or have deformed antlers damaged by screw worm infestations during the velvet stage, or by damage to the pedicel during early growth. The most massive whitetail antlers are the nontypicals, some with total antler mass two or three times that of a normal deer of the same age, habitat, and nutrition. Some nontypicals seem to explode crazily from a deer's skull. Growth in a few captive bucks has been measured at almost one-half inch per day.

Injuries will also affect antler shape and growth. If a deer's right leg is broken, say, the growth of the right antler may be stunted or smaller than the left. I once examined a 3½-year-old buck that had a normal antler on one side and only a

twisted spike on the other. A broadhead arrow point was found embedded in the shoulder on the side of the spike.

Antler Size

While conformation and to some extent size are hereditary, size may depend much more on age and nutrition. A buck's first set of antlers can vary from spikes (one tine or point per side) or forkhorn (two points per side), to as many as ten points (five per side) in rare cases of extremely high nutrition. I have been on well-managed ranches in southern Texas, with deer populations deliberately kept low to produce larger bucks, where many first racks have six points, among a few eight pointers. Phosphorus in the diet is very important in heavier antler growth. Adequate rainfall, or lack of it, can be beneficial or detrimental to a whole summer's crop of antlers.

Second racks will be bigger than the first in spread, usually in number of total points, and in total mass or weight. This increase usually continues until the deer reaches its prime.

This general type of antler formation is typical of the eastern Black Hills in South Dakota, a region shared with mule deer.

The increase may be dramatic on top-quality deer range, but sometimes almost imperceptible where nutrition is very poor. Many whitetailed bucks on poor or marginal range never develop racks that could be considered trophies. Deer country that contains a lot of spikes or forkhorns, especially on older bucks, almost always indicates low-quality or overpopulated range.

HUNTING FOR TROPHIES

The value of keeping deer numbers in check (at range-carrying capacity or below), simply cannot be overemphasized in this or any other work about whitetails. That is doubly true in a culture such as ours where hunting, trophy hunting, is held in fairly high regard.

*These two bucks sport antlers of the so-called high-horned variety. Both are trophy deer, and not very often are two such bucks photographed together. Not long after the picture was taken, the deer were heard fighting out of photo range in dense brush. **Overleaf:** This buck with very high, basket-shaped rack was a dominant breeding animal on a ranch near Choke Canyon State Park in Texas for many years. Many of its male progeny had (and still have) similar antlers.*

Left: *This buck carries an excellent example of very widespread deer antlers, probably twenty-five to twenty-six inches in width; he also is from the south Texas brush country.* **Top:** *This perfectly symmetrical, typical ten-pointer is one of the two finest whitetail bucks I have ever seen or photographed. It was first attracted into camera range near Del Rio, Texas, with a doe decoy doused with doe-in-estrus lure.* **Above:** *Almost as impressive as the buck attracted by the doe decoy, this typical ten-pointer was often seen in the other buck's company. The two may very well have been related, even twin brothers.*

Above: *This is the second of the two largest whitetailed bucks we have ever photographed, this one in north central Texas. At the time it was six and one-half years old, it had thirteen points. After measuring the discarded (shed) antlers, it was figured to score 182 Boone & Crockett points, altogether an extraordinary animal.* **Right:** *The Minnesota buck does not carry the high or widespread antlers of some others illustrated here. But the heavy beams and ten symmetrical points crown the animal very well. Also its large body size makes the antlers seem a little smaller than they are.*

Humans have always hunted animal trophies. More than twenty centuries ago, primitive hunters were scratching records of their trophies on cave walls in Europe. Recently on remote canyon walls in Colorado, hikers discovered depictions of deer with massive antlers (no doubt mule deer) left behind by Anasazi hunters. Not only have men always gone trophy hunting, but they have also been in hot pursuit to bag trophies bigger, more beautiful, more impressive than those captured by anyone else. Statewide, local, and national antler-size contests are held every year across the country, sponsored by beer companies, chambers of commerce, and sporting goods stores. Quite naturally a method to measure and systematically score heads had to be devised. The system accepted everywhere in America today is administered by the national Boone & Crockett Club (250 Station Dr., Missoula, MT 59801). It recognizes three whitetail antler categories: typical, nontypical, plus a special one for the Coues subspecies of the Southwest.

Under Boone & Crockett standards, a buck's antlers are rated (scored) according to a sum of the following dimensions: length of the two main beams, length of all normal points (a point must measure at least one inch to be counted), the greatest inside spread between right and left antlers, the circumference of the main beam. The total of these is called the preliminary score. If the head is typical, deductions are then made for asymmetry—for any difference between the basic measurements of the right and left antlers. Deductions are also made for abnormal points: If there are five points on one side of a rack and four on the other; the length of that extra fifth point is subtracted to determine the final score.

Nontypical or malformed racks are scored in the same way, except that all points, no matter how numerous or where located, are counted in the score.

But scores aside, what exactly is a trophy whitetailed deer? Both average and maximum antler sizes vary greatly from subspecies to subspecies, from state to state, even from county to county. What may be a huge rack in Florida might not raise any eyebrows in Minnesota or Ontario. Besides that, one hunter's standards differ greatly from those of another.

So, like beauty, a trophy head may be mostly in the eye of the beholder. Well-known Texas writer, Byron Dalrymple, has said that "any antler size is directly proportional to the person's adrenaline flow at the time he spots the deer." Although not very scientific, it is a very practical way to measure trophy size.

More to the point and as a rough guide, a true typical whitetail trophy should have at least the following approxi-

mate dimensions: main beams each measuring twenty-four inches around the curve; five or six points per side; inside spread twenty inches between the main beams; a circumference of four and one-half to five inches of the main beam between the burr (base of the antler) and the first point. A whitetail buck of this average size would score between 160 and 165 points. Compare that to the largest known typical antlers (from Minnesota) that scored 207 points.

Contrast that also to the largest known nontypical whitetail, a super Missouri buck found dead in St. Louis County in 1981, which scored 325 7/8 points. To be considered a trophy nontypical rack, the dimensions should be roughly the same as for the typical (just above), but should sport two to three times as many points, for a total score of 180 to 190.

Until 1981, the most massive of all whitetail racks was one with seventy-eight points taken by "Papa" Jeff Benson near Brady, Texas, a century earlier. Controversy still exists whether Benson shot the deer himself, whether he acquired it from someone else, or whether it was a discard he found. In any case anyone can see that rack today, among many other super-trophies, at the Lone Star Brewery's Buckhorn Hall of Fame in San Antonio.

HAS TROPHY-HUNTING GONE TOO FAR?

The desire to own a record or near-record whitetailed deer head has gone to extremes in recent years and has even taken some ugly turns. The fact that racks that rank high in the Boone & Crockett record book command prices up to $20,000 and beyond has encouraged poaching and other chicanery. Experts in plastic are adding extra points to already impressive antlers. And now there are realistic all-plastic copies of originals for sale out there on the market. Deer once considered safe in parks and preserves everywhere are now the targets of very skilled and determined poachers. In 1992 a whole shipment of whitetailed trophy racks was intercepted on its way to Germany, shipper unknown.

In December 1981, Peggy and I photographed a magnificent buck with an immense spread and eighteen points that was living on the ranch of John Leyendecker and Joe Martin III near Laredo, Texas. It was the key animal in a deer-breeding experiment. Although living inside a large fenced area with other deer, the buck was fairly shy of people, and we found it not easy to approach. Less than a month later, at night, poachers entered the area, shot the buck and with it eighteen does and fawns also in the enclosure. All the car-

The side view of a fine twelve-point Columbian buck from Washington state reveals antlers almost as large as this subspecies ever attains.

Judging, or mentally scoring, the size of a whitetailed buck's rack is best done by viewing from directly in front. The opportunity of a side view of the deer only adds to your ability to form a rough calculation.

casses, everything except the trophy buck's head, were left behind. Despite the lengthy investigations by a squad of game wardens, and substantial rewards offered for information, the killers have never been identified or caught.

Recognizing a trophy alive and in the field is as difficult as scoring antlers in the hand with tape and calipers is easy. Few bucks wary enough to reach ripe old trophy age stand still long enough to be carefully observed. Too often a glimpse of the animal moving away, often in shadows or dim light, is the best an observer can hope for. Experience (and the more of it the better) with whitetailed deer on the hoof helps immensely.

The illustrations in this book should help to give a better conception of a trophy or near trophy. Beyond that, keep a few figures in mind. A whitetailed buck with both ears cocked naturally outward and slightly upward measures fifteen to eighteen inches between ear tips. The average healthy buck also measures about fifteen inches thick through the body. So any buck with antlers extending a few inches beyond the ear tips on each side, or wider than the body, is at least a very good specimen.

A panel of the best field judges of whitetail antlers I have ever met (composed of Hefner Appling, Murry Burnham, Murphy Ray, Bob Reagan, Allen Grimland, George Jambers, Jr., and Whitey Ryals) agree on some other rules of thumb. First, try to get a look at the buck from the front, from head-on, for the best evaluation. After checking antler spread, look next at antler height—the length of antler tines. On a true trophy head at least some points should be as long or longer than the ears.

Concentrate on just the one deer in question and disregard any others in the vicinity. Pay no attention to its overall body size or condition. Focus your attention on the points. You should count ten or more. Notice the thickness and color of the antlers; the heavier and darker the beams, the better, although late in the year the antlers may be very light in color. No matter what the purpose, discovering and evaluating whitetail racks in the field can be a fascinating game and an honest test of anybody's outdoor ability. Trophy hunting with a camera is surely the greatest sport of all.

A month after this remarkable eighteen-point buck was photographed near Lardeo, Texas, it was killed by poachers who retrieved only the rack. Trophy poaching is a serious matter in some areas.

Side view of a Texas buck, showing one of the drop points that develop on some older males.

WILDLIFE OF THE WHITETAIL'S WORLD

No matter where it lives, the whitetailed deer is a vital member of the local plant and wildlife community in which each species has an impact and where all species are interdependent. In some parts of their range, deer are important prey of several wild hunters that cannot live without them. But countless other creatures from bees and hummingbirds to mice and beavers affect whitetail lives in more subtle ways. Whitetails also have an impact on other creatures.

The bees and hummingbirds, for example, pollinate a good many plants on which deer depend. But a plague of mice in an area can nibble and wipe out a year's crop of seedlings that deer would require for future browse. With a few night's work, a family of beavers can impound a creek and flood a meadow where does and fawns traditionally spent summer after summer. Another larger, taller native deer, the moose, often is serious competition for the limited food that is available throughout a northern winter.

If you come across a whitetail feeding around the edge of a weedy pond in the midwestern United States, the odds are one in three that the animal is being infected by another predator almost impossible to see, the larvae of a liver fluke. A snail serves as the intermediate host. The larvae enter the deer's body on vegetation, lay eggs in its liver, and reenter the water in deer droppings, completing their life cycle. Fortunately this microscopic predator does not too seriously affect the health of its host. But it is an example of a creature's dependence on deer, as far west as Oregon and as far south as Texas, where more than half of the deer examined carried the flukes.

Under some conditions, almost every species of meat-eater that shares the whitetail's range will feed on deer. The list would have to include cougars, coyotes, wolves, bears, bobcats, foxes, wolverines, and golden eagles. Even fishers, foxes, lynx, and ravens have been seen killing or trying to bring down fawns. The severe winters in the north and seasonal famines elsewhere make even adult deer more vulnerable to the smaller predators.

WOLVES AND WHITETAILS

Historically wolves along with cougars were the primary controllers of deer populations throughout the whitetail's range: Mexican wolves (*Canis lupus baileyi*) in parts of Arizona, New Mexico, west Texas, and Mexico; red wolves (*Canis niger*) south of the Ohio River and westward to Oklahoma and east Texas; and gray or timber wolves (*Canis lupus*) almost everywhere else. Now, unless reintroduction programs are successful, Mexican and red wolves are probably extinct in the wild, but gray wolves and whitetails still share range across parts of southern Canada, in northern Wisconsin, Michigan, and Minnesota, and most recently in northwestern Montana, where the wolves are recolonizing from adjacent Alberta. Before North America was settled, whitetailed deer supplied the venison the wolves of many regions needed to survive. But their effect on deer populations today is minimal.

In recent years, many studies of wolf predation have been undertaken, most notably by U.S. Fish and Wildlife Service biologist L. David Mech, who has devoted his life to this work

Raccoon tracks are commonly found mixed with deer tracks in forests and wetlands all across America. **Overleaf:** *Porcupines live widely in deer habitats across North America. They gnaw on and recycle dropped deer antlers for the abundant minerals they contain.*

Wherever the ranges of the two species overlap, wolves are swift, skillful predators of whitetailed deer in all seasons, but with special emphasis on winter. This buck was struck by a car in the Montana-Alberta area, and the carcass was recycled by a pair of wolves.

and has virtually lived with wolves for long periods. He concludes that during summer, wolves prey mostly on fawns. In winter they kill older fawns and deer more than five years of age. Mech notes, too, that wolves typically capture a disproportionate number of adult bucks and whitetails with abnormalities. In winter, fawns carry the lowest fat supplies and many of the bucks, already left weakened and drained by the rut, often suffer from arthritis in their hind leg joints, making them easier to kill.

Wolves are notorious travelers, always hunting; they must devote much of their lives to this pursuit. To watch them soon reveals why they capture only certain weaker classes of deer. When a wolf pack or family senses or sees a deer, they try to creep or stalk closer without flushing it, which is never easy. A whitetail's senses are just as keen as a wolf's, and as soon as it detects them, the deer will flee. Wolves immediately take up the chase, but seemingly only half-heartedly (as if testing) and usually for just a few minutes, since under most conditions a healthy whitetail can outrun any wolf. But if the deer seems weak or falters, the wolves, sensing some weakness, step up the pace. Mech knows of one chase that lasted for two hours and covered thirteen miles.

Deep soft snow may hinder wolves even more than it does deer, which tend to bound up and out of the snow while the wolves sink and plunge through. But the pads of wolves give them much more support on packed snow than the sharp hooves of the whitetails, and the advantage shifts greatly to the wolves in late winter. At this time, for short periods, a crust covers the snow that is thick enough to hold the wild dogs, but will not support the deer, whose feet stab through the surface with each step.

Whitetailed deer are good swimmers and in summer will often take to the water of northern lakes to escape both insects and wolves. It usually works, even though wolves will occasionally try to swim in pursuit. Although there is one record of a wolf catching and killing a deer in freezing water, there is growing evidence that deer living on islands, peninsulas, and North Woods lakeshores have higher survivability than those elsewhere, presumably because they can flee to the protective waters when pressed.

The extreme tenacity and endurance of whitetailed deer is illustrated by the experience of Minnesota pilot-biologist Michael Nelson in November, 1982. Nelson was flying over a lake-studded part of the Superior National Forest in the northern part of the state, tracking a pack of seven wolves, one of which was radio-collared to study its movements. Nelson saw

Coyotes are too often considered as wanton killers of game, especially of deer, as well as livestock. But this super dog is really an opportunist that survives largely on smaller creatures.

that the wolves were running around a partially frozen lake, apparently to intercept a deer that was swimming on a parallel course. His watch read 10:45 A.M. The temperature was below freezing. When about one hundred yards from shore, the deer must have spotted the wolves and, realizing its predicament, turned to swim back across the lake, a distance of two miles.

Nelson had to leave the chase taking place below him to refuel, but returned three and one-half hours later to find the whitetail still in the water and the wolves still stalking from the nearest point on shore. Eventually, four and one-half hours after Nelson first encountered the drama in progress, the wolves caught the deer in shallow water where it came, exhausted, to rest. Of all land animals, only polar bears could be expected to survive so long under stress in freezing water.

Occasionally wolves pay for their predation. Biologists have found a surprising number of wolf skulls fractured from severe blows, often by moose hooves, but many by much smaller whitetails. Late in 1983 and also in the Superior National Forest, a forester discovered the carcass of a seventy-five-pound female wolf, in good body condition except for fatal injuries around the head and neck. Nearby was a nine-point whitetailed buck, also dead.

Tom Pearson was able to reconstruct what had happened.

A group of four wolves had "jumped" the deer, which could not outrun them in deep snow. Although they managed to kill and partially eat the animal before being themselves surprised by Pearson, the wolf family was reduced to three in the process.

Twice I've found wolves feeding on deer (one of which was a mule deer), but in both instances, it turned out, the deer had been struck by cars and had managed to drag themselves a short distance into the brush. I do not know if the deer were alive or dead when the wolves found them, but both were being quickly recycled. In one instance a male and female pair of wolves dragged the carcass a quarter-mile away after one feeding.

One point about the wolf–whitetailed deer relationship must be made. The two were living together in balance for centuries before the wolves were almost eliminated from most of their original range. In fact, the predators assured the health of the deer herds by culling the unfit. Deer and wolves are still getting along in the greatly diminished range that the two cohabit. As a result of his most recent deer studies, Dave Mech has concluded that it may occasionally be necessary to control wolf populations where either they become too numerous or

Above: *The mountain lion or cougar hunts in scattered areas of western whitetail range and is capable of catching mature deer as well as fawns.*
Left: *This young coyote seems uncertain about what to do with the desiccated head of a deer from an old winter kill it has uncovered.*

the deer numbers too few.

THE "DEER CAT"

Contrary to common belief, cougars, like wolves, have no detrimental effect on the deer herds that share their also-diminished range. Cougars (sometimes called the "deer tiger" or "cat" and also known as "mountain lion" or "puma") have fared somewhat better than wolves in the United States, probably because of their more secretive and solitary lifestyles.

Maurice Hornocker of Moscow, Idaho, is another of the modern biologists who has learned most about the species by virtually living and camping along their trails for long periods in the central Idaho wilderness. Using hounds to unravel their tracks, Hornocker live-captured, tagged, and radio-collared more than a hundred mountain lions. And his conclusions about them were remarkably similar to those of Dave Mech about wolves. Cougars are opportunists that prey on deer that are easiest to stalk and kill. In the process the big tawny cats are sometimes injured themselves.

A cougar's instinct or strategy is to stalk upwind to within charging range of a deer. This distance is at most fifty yards, and usually much less. Then, in a sudden, swift rush, it bounds onto a deer's back or neck, biting into the spine and probably trying to break it, with a clawed paw grasping the face. A veteran cougar hunter told me that lions usually try to rush at deer from above, from upslope, maybe to knock the animal down and have it rolling before actually grabbing it. After feeding, first on liver and entrails, the carcass might be dragged away to deep shade and concealment where it is blanketed with debris until the cat again feeds on it.

More and more whitetailed deer are moving westward, for the first time invading the last strongholds of the mountain lion, as in west Texas, Wyoming, northern Idaho, Montana, and Alberta. So probably there is still much more to learn about the relationship and how it will evolve.

COYOTES

Perhaps the most controversial North American mammal is the coyote, but not only or always because they can prey on our most popular game species. Once purely a western native despised by stockmen (especially sheepmen), the coyote has expanded its range all across North America to the Atlantic Coast. Hunted and killed by any means for the past half-century, coyotes now are also considered a nuisance in the East, even amid suburbia along the Atlantic seaboard. If any native wild creature can be considered the smartest, the most adaptable, the best survivor of civilization, it has to be this "song dog" or "brush wolf."

Coyotes do account for many whitetailed fawn fatalities nationwide (perhaps the most of any wild hunters) or what might seem an abnormal toll in some areas. Locally in Texas, coyotes are credited—blamed by landowners and hunters—with the early death of eight in every ten fawns born. Actually, Texas fawn survival varies from as low as 7 percent during droughts to as high as 70 percent, not the 80 percent that some would attribute entirely to coyotes. Furthermore, mortality during droughts is a result of more than coyote predation alone. Fawns also starve to death.

But during the 1980s when whitetail populations throughout Texas hovered close to (or even well above) the carrying capacity of their range, the coyotes seemed to be taking only a surplus, the fawns not needed to maintain a sustainable population. Some Texas biologists believe that coyote predation is always greatest on land that is being overgrazed by domestic livestock where protective cover for fawns is very thin and other coyote prey is scarce.

Often I have watched coyotes (one alone to as many as a family of four hunting together) try to catch mule deer, including fawns several months old. But I've never seen a stalk succeed, or even come close to it. Coyote predation of whitetails crowded into winter yards is often reported as heavy and certainly does occur. But as often as not, investigating biologists find free-roaming house dogs to be the culprits. They also find that the venison in most coyote scats comes from eating winter-killed deer. Michigan biologists found coyotes digging into snow banks two feet deep to retrieve deer carcasses. Nationwide and over the long term, coyotes are not nearly the culprits—the fawn predators—that too many believe them to be.

BLACK BEARS AND BOBCATS

Not so long ago, defining whitetailed deer range would also be describing black bear country. Although it is still true, bear numbers in the eastern two-thirds of the United States and Canada have been drastically reduced. Although a rare few black bears may have developed the habit or ability to prey on whitetail fawns in early summer, the species cannot be considered a serious predator, or even much more than modest competition. Black bears are omnivores, rather than carnivores, which seasonally prefer some of the same forbs, berries, and nuts that a whitetail also relishes.

Together with the coyote, the widespread bobcat is a small- to medium-sized predator capable of killing small deer, but it is normally is only a very small threat to strong and healthy

The range of the black bear in the United States and Canada coincides almost exactly with that of whitetailed deer. Wandering bruins will find a few fawns every spring and eat them, but while deer are coping with winter above ground, the bears are hibernating underneath.

Wherever they still cling to survival south of the United States border, jaguars prey on deer whenever they have the opportunity. But probably deer are never important prey for these spotted cats.

The bobcat was found near the partially eaten carcass of a deer in late winter. Death may have come from starvation or from a wolf kill.

adults. They could conceivably take a toll of winter-weakened deer, and recently there have been scattered reports of bobcats being a real menace to the much larger deer, especially in the Northeast.

Judging from signs left in the snow, the cat's tactic is to circle a bedded deer herd, watching for one unwilling or unable to stand up, then to pounce on it and seize it by the head with forepaws. Some terrified deer might be able to run and brush the cat off against trees and brush, but the cats are amazingly strong and could, in some cases, prevail. With the deer finally down for good, the bobcat will stay close to its frozen carcass for two weeks or more, guarding it until every scrap of venison has been stripped away. Like wolves and many predators, bobcats tend to gorge when all at once a large supply of meat becomes available. Survival is just as uncertain for the killers as it is for the prey.

OBSERVING THE WHITETAIL'S WORLD

Many of my richest outdoor experiences have been the unexpected encounters with a myriad of other creatures when roaming in a whitetail woods with camera, blind, and tripod. Even the oldest, wariest whitetails tend not to look upward very often because throughout their evolution danger has always lurked at ground level rather than overhead. So I often watch from trees limbs or build blinds in the branches beside busy game trails because most deer do not notice me there until they are extremely close. An important bonus for a person in a tree in good deer country is the certainty of spotting a lot more than just deer.

The first bobcat and first wild turkey I ever saw, almost a half-century ago, were both from hiding places in tree crowns. Those turkeys were on Blackbeard Island, Georgia, but since then I have had intimate views of many hundreds from South Carolina to south Texas in the same manner and in good whitetail habitat. As with black bears, the range of turkeys coincides almost exactly with that of whitetailed deer, except that turkeys are faring much better than bruins in the last part of the twentieth century.

There is no better way to count many residents of the whitetail's world than while hidden quietly in an elevated deer blind in typical southern Texas brush country. The vigil should begin before daybreak and, after a recess around noon, continue until dusk. Nowhere outside of some East African national parks or in Yellowstone National Park have I seen more creatures in one spot than on the ranches of my friends Hefner Appling in LaSalle County and George T. Jambers, Jr., in Liveoak County.

Both ranches are unique in that they are managed specifically to produce trophy whitetailed bucks for hunting and photography, and because about ten thousand acres of optimum whitetail habitat are enclosed within ten-foot-high

The American mink is a familiar resident along many if not most of the streams that drain whitetail country.

In some areas deer numbers and deer health may be regulated as much by a bumper crop of cottontail rabbits as by any predators. This is because rabbits eat many if not most of the same plant foods on which deer depend.

Although they are not important predators of deer, alligators lurk in swampier deer country of the Southeast and no doubt will capture an occasional, unwary whitetail.

deerproof fences. On the Appling ranch elevated blinds have been erected for deer watching at intervals above the brush. Thin strips, called senderos (which incidentally is the name of the ranch), have been cleared, and radiate outward from the towers. Occasionally these openings are baited with grain or high nutrition pellets. A cameraman sitting in a tower for a few days can expose a lot more film than he had ever intended.

Javelinas—collared peccaries—are usually among the first to find and freeload on the grain bonanza. One morning a great horned owl flew to perch very near my hiding place and soon was being tormented by crows and a trio of Harris' hawks. A coyote drifted ghostlike across a sendero only minutes after an armadillo had passed traveling in the opposite direction. Cottontails and jackrabbits were always on the scene. Other blind occupants here saw a cougar on one cold, but indelible morning.

Late one still afternoon I watched two whitetail bucks browsing slowly in my direction along the edge of a sendero, and I focused my camera on the nearest of them. Then barely twenty-five feet in front of the buck I saw a covey of bobwhite quail work their way toward a scattering of grain. After watching the birds for a few moments, I turned my attention again toward the deer, and in that split second, a bobcat catapulted

out of the brush and knocked down one of the quail as it flushed. Unfortunately my camera was still focused on the deer that also vanished into the lengthening shadows.

In the Southeast the whitetail shares its range with a slightly different cast of creatures, from wood warblers and wading birds to raccoons, opossums, diamondback rattlesnakes, and alligators. I do not know if whitetails fear rattlesnakes, but many observers insist that deer give rattlers a wide berth when they meet, which isn't surprising. There are also reports, always of does, killing rattlesnakes by stomping on them with sharp hooves. A Georgia beekeeper once wrote me that he had seen a deer circling a place on the ground, hidden from his view, and then striking at it with all four feet the way a gray fox in that same habitat would pounce on a mouse. The man investigated and found a still alive, but badly punctured, diamondback about five feet long.

Almost certainly large alligators capture a few deer as they cross streams, cypress swamps, and bayous of the South where the reptiles are numerous. On the other hand, we have photographed whitetails wading (even swimming) and feeding in all these places with no more than normal caution.

In the Northeast and northern Midwest, it would be impossible to wander far without flushing ruffed grouse or woodcock. Groundhogs whistle from den entrances around the

In many places, deer habitat has actually been created by dam-building beavers, while elsewhere, deer habitat has been flooded. Deer browse the lush edges of beaver ponds. In time the ponds fill with silt and become meadows where deer and other creatures live.

fringes of woodlots. Farther west whitetails are beginning to pass from ruffed grouse into blue grouse country, and farthest north to invade sharptail and spruce grouse range. During recent times I watched whitetails and their closest cousins, mule deer, browsing not too far apart in three widely separated locales: the haunting Trans-Pecos of West Texas; in Montana's cooler, greener Flathead River valley; and in my own back pasture in Montana's Paradise Valley of the Yellowstone River. If they noticed one another, it wasn't evident.

All across southern Canada tracks and trails of the snowshoe hare everywhere cross those of whitetailed deer. Red or pine squirrels have time and again alerted me to a deer's approach before I could see or hear them. In deciduous forests everywhere gray and fox squirrels patrol the world just overhead. They also come to the ground to compete with deer for fall's irregular crop of acorns and beechnuts.

I am firmly convinced that the deer's most serious competitor is not a native creature at all, but the feral hog which now runs freely and widely over the southern half of the United States. So much do deer and hogs depend on the same foods year around that whenever the more aggressive hogs proliferate, the whitetails do not have a chance. In fact by their rooting, digging, and gorging, hogs can reduce the floor of a green whitetail woods to a foul-smelling wasteland. Add to this the growing evidence that hogs also will consume any small fawns they find and they may be far better at this than coyotes. Pigs belong confined in pig pens, never in the wild. A whitetail herd can prosper—or at least cope with—what we might call natural predation. But when an extra prolific element such as the feral hog is introduced, the old balance can be lost.

This much is certain: The whitetail lives on some of the most beautiful, most accessible landscapes of our country, another reason we should stubbornly protect our precious natural environment everywhere at any cost.

The lynx is an increasingly threatened species native to the same woodland as the northern whitetailed deer. Although lynxes capture a few very young fawns in spring, they do not have great impact on deer numbers anywhere.

Opossums inhabit the same trees of the Southeast beneath which whitetails feed and bed. They also eat some of the same wild fruits and berries.

Left: The javelina or collared peccary shares whitetail country in west Texas, Arizona, and northern Mexico. In times of drought, it may become a serious competitor for food. **Right:** European wild boars, feral hogs, and hybrids of these are very prolific and in some areas of the South can be very detrimental to deer herds by monopolizing important foods such as acorns, destroying habitat, and even killing fawns.

Above: *Gambel's quail lives with the whitetail in the southwestern United States.* **Right:** *The wild turkey is another species with a range that almost exactly coincides with that of whitetailed deer. It also shares an innate wariness of humans and relishes many of the same foods—acorns for example—as deer.*

OTHER NORTH AMERICAN DEER

The whitetail is only one, and the smallest, of six native North American deer of the family Cervidae. The others are the moose, elk or wapiti, caribou, mule deer, and the blacktailed deer. The whitetail's range overlaps all but one of these, the caribou, sometimes over vast areas, elsewhere just barely. In addition, a number of exotic deer species have been introduced into the United States and Canada from Asia and Europe. Some of these are already serious competitors, or have the potential to seriously compete with the whitetails, if not to replace them.

MULE AND BLACKTAILED DEER

When Europeans began to settle North America, mule deer, *Odocoileus hemionus*, lived in the vast wilderness east of the West Coast's Cascade Mountains and west of the one-hundred-degree meridian, or roughly west of the Mississippi River and in what is now Manitoba, Alberta, British Columbia, and the Yukon. The thin Pacific coastal strip west of the Cascades was occupied by the closely related blacktailed deer, *Odocoileus hemionus columbianus* (California north to southern British Columbia) or *Odocoileus hemionus sitkensis* (of northern British Columbia and Alaska). Most often blacktails are regarded as a subspecies of mule deer, although the opposite may be nearer the truth. Like the whitetail, both of these western animals can trace their lineage far back to the same piglike Pleistocene ancestor.

Mule deer are named for their unusually large ears, but resemble mules in no other way. They are not quite as swift and graceful in motion as whitetails, perhaps because they tend to average heavier. We have no idea of their original numbers, but turn-of-the-century writer Ernest Thompson Seton estimated the mule deer population to have been ten million before the West was "won," or lost, depending on how you regard "progress." Many modern biologists think the actual number may have been only half that. The greatest numbers today live in Colorado, Wyoming, Utah, Nevada, Idaho, Montana, Alberta, and British Columbia.

The journals of early American explorers and trappers seldom mention mule deer, possibly because they seemed insignificant among the vast herds of bison, the elk, and the pronghorn antelope. Plains Indians did not consider mule deer meat and fat to be as desirable as a bison's, but nonetheless never wasted it. Old accounts describe how mule deer buckskin, scraped very thin and stretched, could be used as translucent window panes in winter dwellings.

Mule vs. Whitetailed Deer

Today, mule and whitetailed deer ranges are overlapping more and more as whitetails colonize westward. Whitetails seem to be following major river drainages such as the Missouri-Yellowstone upstream to establish themselves on irrigated croplands. Not nearly as adaptable, "muleys" remain much more a wilderness species, especially of the western mountain wilderness. There is now evidence that mule deer and whitetailed deer can and occasionally do interbreed where their ranges overlap.

Mule deer are the closest cousins of the whitetails, and the two now share some western ranges. The larger mule deer seem to be slowly retreating ahead of invading, more adaptable whitetails, especially where humans alter the landscape.

It is fairly easy to distinguish the mule deer from their eastern relatives. Muleys' tails are distinctive. Whitetails wave their pennant-shaped tails when alarmed or when running to clearly expose the pure white underneath. Often this is all a person sees in a dark evergreen woodland. Mule deer seldom raise their shorter, ropelike tails, which are dull white with black tips. Blacktailed deer have dark brown or black tails, darker toward the ends. A mule deer's metatarsal glands on the hind legs between hock and hoof are covered with brown hair; a whitetail's are covered with white hair.

The antler conformation is also distinctive in mule bucks. Contrasted to the typical whitetail rack, with opposing main beams from which extra points grow upward, the main beams of both mules and blacktails branch into two beams, each of which then branches again. The racks of mule deer tend to grow heavier, more massive than whitetails', commensurate with their larger body dimensions. Mule deer males also often grow huge non-typical racks with many points, forks, and drop points, which are either grotesque or very impressive, depending on your viewpoint.

Another important difference between America's two most common deer is evident the instant a mule deer begins to run. Instead of the whitetail's fluid motion, mule deer bound away in a unique, stiff-legged gait, seeming to strike downward and backward with all four feet at once. This pogo-stick bounce is deceptive; the animals can cover twenty feet or more in a bound and quickly disappear into the distance. Some mule deer live in more wide open country than most whitetails, but otherwise the life histories of the two are similar.

From my standpoint as an incurable trophy hunter with a camera, I've learned two important facts about mule bucks. The first is that the biggest bachelors spend summers and early falls in the loftiest, least accessible parts of their range—in high, lovely alpine landscapes where the air is thin. Second, except for mountain goats, they are at least as sure-footed at the top of their range as bighorned sheep or any other large mammals of the American West.

ELK OR WAPITI

Except for caribou, the American elk (*Cervus canadensis*) was probably the most widespread of all hooved animals when Columbus reached the New World. Their range then stretched from California to Pennsylvania and the Carolinas, from Mexico north and east to the valley of southeast Canada's St. Lawrence River. Half of this transcontinental area was also occupied by whitetails. But expanding human settlement had eliminated almost all the elk east of the Mississippi River by

Both photos: *Superficially, the blacktailed deer of the Pacific Coast resembles the whitetail more than any of the whitetail's "cousins" and can easily be mistaken for it. The former has black (rather than brown) hair on top of the tail, and the male's antler formation is rather like that of a mule deer, of which it may be a subspecies. The photo in the lower right is of a blacktailed doe with twin fawns.*

the early 1800s. Today wild whitetails and wapiti meet only in scattered sites along the base of the Rocky Mountains and in southwestern Canada. The range of the elk now coincides much more with that of mule deer and blacktails.

With good reason, hunters rank wapitis high among the most desirable of trophies. A bull's antlers, with multiple points spreading more than four feet tip to tip, can weigh as much as fifty pounds by the time the animal is prime at five and one-half years old. Fully grown, the bull will stand four and one-half to five feet tall at the shoulder and weigh, depending on locality and nutrition, between 550 and 800 pounds. Fully grown cows in late summer weigh from 450 to 600 pounds, about four times the weight of an average whitetail.

The largest trophy elk I ever photographed was in north-western Washington, of the Olympic or Roosevelt subspecies. Close to it in size were some of the bulls of Jasper National Park, Alberta. Late in August and still in the velvet, the Washington state bull's great antlers had eight points on one side and seven on the other. An elk rack is considered a genuine trophy—a royal—if it has six points per side.

In Canada, elk are most abundant in the mountain wilderness areas of southern Alberta and British Columbia. As for the population in the United States, more elk live today in Wyoming than in any other state, and a good percentage of these spend the winter in Jackson Hole, on the National Elk Refuge. Here it is possible to count as many as eight thousand animals at one time. Originally this herd migrated from summer range in what is now Yellowstone National Park and elsewhere in northwestern Wyoming toward winter ranges south of Jackson Hole. But their migration route was blocked long ago by a town and by ranching, so they are fed by humans over the winter and held on the refuge. Summers are spent in high and cool mountain meadows where calves are born in late May or early June. Mature bulls keep their distance from cow and calf herds, devoting the warm months to growing those splendid antlers and accumulating fat on their bodies.

The Elk Rut

If the autumn rut of the whitetailed deer is busy and sometimes exciting, the annual rut of the elk is absolutely spectacular, often nonstop for a period of two or three weeks in late September. Northern Yellowstone National Park is the best of places to see it.

As elk herds begin to move gradually downward from summer ranges to lower elevations, bachelor bulls "invade" the cow groups, each bull trying to separate as many females as possible into his own harem for breeding. Normally the

stronger bulls assemble the biggest harems, which may consist of as many as twenty-five or thirty cows. Lesser bulls get two or three or none at all. But what follows is an almost constant, day-and-night turmoil in which major bulls are forced to round up restive harem members, to posture, bugle, threaten, pursue, and often to drive off rival bulls. Some of these encounters are savage and loud, the sound of crashing antlers heard from a great distance.

Probably the most unique feature of the elk rut is the frequent shrill bugling of the males. In all the outdoors few sights and sounds are more stirring. But exactly why a bull bugles remains a mystery, a subject of myth and misconceptions. One misconception is that the calliopelike bugle, plus grunting, often answered by another male, is a challenge to other bulls. But more likely it is the staking of a claim or an invitation to other females to come and join up with a winner.

Another myth is that the age and size of a bull can be measured by the tone or volume, or both, of a bull's bugle. Untrue. While a thin squeak might distinguish a yearling from a male grown hoarse with age, volume seems more a matter of vocal capacity and inspiration than of anything else. By the time the elk rut winds down, bulls bugle less and less frequently, and finally fall entirely silent. When heavy snow begins to fall, the rut ends and America's second largest deer settle down to survive grim winter, just as the smaller whitetails do.

MOOSE

Moose (*Alces alces*) not only are the largest deer in America, but also in the entire world. They are too often described as ugly, ungainly, or ponderous and lumbering. I see them instead as handsome and perfectly adapted to survive in the habitat they occupy today.

Any seeming ungainliness is deceptive. The long legs and pistonlike strides are a powerful combination. A healthy moose can travel far and fast with ease through the same marsh in which other large creatures would flounder or would avoid altogether. Deep snows that drain the strength or even immobilize a whitetail are easily negotiated by a full-grown moose. I do not believe that moose become easily irritated or are as aggressive as is often written, but when they do get mad, stay out of their path and that of those pounding hooves.

Nor is the long "homely" face and drooping muzzle a handicap to a moose. In many regions the species is more aquatic than any other deer, and these facial characteristics enable a moose to browse selectively on submerged vegetation, even while the animal stands flank-deep in a beaver pond or bog. With only eyes and ears above water, it can

Elk, also called wapiti, share many of the same geographical areas in the West with deer, but very rarely the same specific habitats within those areas. Averaging three to four times as large as whitetails, they are in no way competitors.

watch and listen for danger as its dines. Out of water the same generous muzzle allows a moose to neatly strip the tender green leaves from willow shoots, its favorite food. So a moose's muzzle is definitely utilitarian.

The body of an adult is deep and heavy, with long dark brown to black outer hair. The long legs are lighter, usually grayish. The fine hairy undercoat hidden beneath the outer hair enables this species to endure bitterly cold winters by preventing loss of too much body heat. At the same time the dark color absorbs solar warmth. Moose have bedded down in my backyard during brutal snow storms for many hours, even days at a time, without having to move, completely covered (except for eyes and ears) by the snow.

Another peculiarity of moose is mystifying and deceptive. The same black bull that one day lumbers through a dry forest, crunching debris under over-sized hooves and breaking off tree limbs in its path, can on another day pass silently, even ghostlike through that same timber.

Depending on the taxonomist, there are three or (probably) four moose subspecies living on this continent. *Alces alces giqas* of Alaska and the Yukon is the largest. *Alces alces shirasi* of Wyoming and the northern Rockies is the smallest.

In between are *Alces alces andersoni* of western Canada and *Alces alces americana* of eastern Canada and New England. A Wyoming bull can reach a prime-of-life weight of twelve hundred pounds. A full-grown Alaskan bull standing seven feet at the shoulder could exceed a ton.

Bulls anywhere need strong necks to support the heaviest antlers known in the animal kingdom. The palmated racks of some trophy Alaskan bulls have spanned more than six feet and weighed well over seventy-five pounds. It is almost inconceivable that such a mass of bone, that might exceed the weight of a human skeleton, could be grown during a single, three- to four-month season, and summer after summer. By contrast, it takes sixteen to twenty years for a human skeleton to reach full size.

All North American moose are less gregarious than elk and caribou, or even than mule deer, which are usually classified as herd animals. But they are not really as solitary a species as is often written. Throughout our long wandering in moose country, across wilderness North America at all seasons, we have more often found two or more together than just one moose alone. What is more, the moose is the only other large animal that might live amicably among whitetailed

The largest member of the deer family, Cervidae, in North America and on earth, the moose is the one large mammal that might be encountered living and feeding amicably in close proximity to whitetails. Still, the two are competitors for available food. When one species becomes very abundant, the other usually declines. Moose are the stronger survivors of bitter winters.

deer, or vice versa. I have seen the two browsing almost side by side in Ontario's Algonquin Provincial Park.

CARIBOU

More than a million caribou (*Rangifer tarandus*) today roam the coldest, northernmost reaches of this continent, across northern Canada and much of Alaska, but this is a fraction of their original numbers. There are four very similar subspecies: *Rangifer tarandus caribou* of mainland trans-Canada; *Rangifer tarandus groenlandicus* of northern Canada and Greenland; *Rangifer tarandus granti* of Alaska; *Rangifer tarandus pearyi* of Canadian far Arctic islands. Except for the last, which is cream colored, the others are not distinguishable in the field. In addition, the reindeer of northern Europe, *Rangifer tarandus tarandus*, was introduced into Alaska. Whitetailed deer and caribou ranges probably do not overlap, but if at all, only in the wild region just north of the Great Lakes.

This Arctic deer of lonely northern wilderness appears ungainly on first impression. It has a thick muzzle, a maned neck, and broad hooves concave underneath, designed for endless travel over snow, muskeg, and tundra. Bodies of bulls are brown in summer with chest and legs being darker. Rump, belly, and tail are white. The neck is gray, but in early autumn this begins to turn white. By winter the entire body, covered with dense, insulating hair, becomes grizzled. A caribou of winter, especially a mature bull, is a far more striking animal than it was six months earlier.

Caribou are the most impervious to cold and the most amphibious of all the deer. Of all hooved animals, only caribou and musk oxen are able to withstand the winters of total darkness in some of the lowest temperatures on earth, on a meager diet of lichens. When winter is replaced by summer's total daylight and Arctic waterways thaw, caribou readily swim lakes and rivers during the migrations or to escape from wolves. Adults can maintain a speed of three to four miles per hour in the water.

A caribou's life is one of incessant travel, of long annual migrations from wintering areas to calving grounds in the spring and back again. One band, the Porcupine Herd, is an international group that for countless millennia has been traveling between Alaska and the Yukon. Biologists today remain baffled about what triggers migration.

A unique characteristic among mammals is the clicking sound made by caribou as they travel. When a herd of hundreds is moving along rapidly, the sound of a thousand or more hooves clicking is unearthly on an otherwise silent tundra.

Also unique in the deer family are the antlers grown by

129

caribou cows, which are smaller than bull antlers, but which are retained longer into the winter. However, there are few more splendid spectacles in the far northern wilderness than that of a mature caribou bull, white mane blowing in an Arctic wind, displaying scarlet antlers against a blue or threatening black sky. The antlers are red for a short time just after the velvet has peeled away. A trophy bull's antlers can exceed three feet in height, with long flattened or palmate beams containing as many as forty total points. One, or rarely two, palmate brow tines (or "shovels") extend straight out between the eyes and over the muzzle.

The rutting season of the caribou may be even more noisy and violent than that of the elk. Bulls stop eating altogether. With necks swollen to twice the normal size, the bachelor friendships of summer dissolve as bulls turn on one another in furious contests of strength. At the peak of the rut, the violence level becomes so great that some males may be maimed or killed. A stiff price must be paid for entering this annual male competition to breed.

At rut's end, the bodies of larger bulls are drained of fat reserves and their body weights reduced by as much as 25 percent. Antlers fall off, and this suddenly relegates them to second-class status. The older cows are now dominant in the herd. Just surviving the winter is an ordeal that all do not live through. Wolves are always stalking the caribou, taking the easiest targets and seeing that only the fittest bulls survive.

EXOTIC DEER IN NORTH AMERICA
Axis Deer

In all the world there may be no more elegant deer—no ungulate more striking—than the chital, spotted, or axis deer, *Axis axis*, of southern Asia. Whitetail fawns are beautifully spotted at birth, but chital retain their cream-spotted cinnamon coats all their lives. An adult stag stands three feet at the shoulder and is six feet from nose to tip of tail. At about two hundred pounds, it is heavier than an average whitetail buck. It is no wonder that the legionnaires of ancient Rome brought back these spotted deer, along with the gold, tapestries, and other plunder, to live in the world's first zoos or game parks.

The singularly beautiful axis deer are only one of many species of deer that have been imported from around the globe and released into North American habitats. This introduction is at the very best a mixed blessing, both to such natives as the whitetail, and to the overall environment. Over thousands of years whitetails have evolved to live in relative harmony with the elk and other indigenous deer, as well as with the predators that hunt them. The combination usually re-

The range of the northernmost whitetails on this continent might just barely overlap the range (and southernmost migration points) of barren ground caribou. All of these are males in the velvet, except the one with reddened antlers; he has just shed his velvet.

mains in good balance. But getting along with most of the aliens may be another matter altogether for whitetails.

Spotted deer are more herd animals than either whitetails or mule deer. Both in India and on Texas ranches, I have found them living in groups of forty to fifty. During very dry seasons the herds merge into super-herds as they strike out in search of water, where they congregate until the drought breaks.

Except for coyotes, which might kill a fawn or two occasionally, axis deer have met no serious predators where they are now established in America. But losses to coyotes are hardly measurable because this species is so prolific that it can soon outnumber any enemies. There are at least some animals in each herd that can (and do) breed throughout the year. Many times in south Texas I have watched whitetails in the velvet grazing in the same field beside chital bucks with polished antlers (who are further along in their breeding cycle), as well as with fawns of various ages. Wherever their numbers are not strictly limited by hunting or culling, axis deer soon crowd out native competition and seriously overgraze their American pastures.

The woodland caribou is a disappearing species, and is classified as endangered in the United States, with a shrinking range in the northern Rocky Mountains that whitetailed deer may invade.

The boom in introducing horned as well as antlered exotics—and it *is* currently a boom—probably began in 1929 when Robert Kleberg, Sr., of the King Ranch in Texas, bought eight Indian nilgai, or blue bulls, from a defunct circus in Corpus Christi. The animals' descendants still live on the King Ranch—by the hundreds. During the 1940s and the 1950s other Texans began to collect exotics, which are now commonly called Texotics, to free them mostly on ranches in the central Texas Hill Country. Dick Friedrich was a pioneer at this, but in the early 1950s Charles Schreiner III began to heavily stock his YO Ranch near Mountain Home with many Asian and African species, mostly for trophy-hunting purposes.

Today Texotics are living everywhere in the Hill Country, as well as elsewhere in Texas, the Southwest, and scattered other locales on the continent. In 1984 a census by the Texas Department of Parks and Wildlife placed the number of exotics in the state at about 120,000 (of which about 38,000 were axis deer). But most landowners in the Texotic business regard that figure as too conservative; instead they estimated that two to three times that number would be closer to fact in 1992.

Sika

Another common alien is the sika, *Cervus nippon*, a deer of the Far East, where thirteen similar subspecies are native, from the Chinese district of Tibet to the Japanese island of Okinawa and from Vietnam to Manchuria in northern China. Although a few collectors and North American zoos maintain pure subspecies, the origin of most sikas now roaming America has been lost. What we have is a prolific, dark, sometimes faintly spotted hybrid deer, slightly smaller on the average than whitetails. Except through selective breeding, they do not normally grow as fine trophy racks as whitetails and axis deer do. But nonetheless they are extremely competitive animals.

The implications of stocking sikas in the wild first became clear with a 1971 study by Texas deer researchers on the Kerr Wildlife Management Area. There in a ninety-six-acre, escape-proof pasture, they released two sika bucks and four sika does, as well as two whitetail bucks and four whitetail does—six of each species. The animals were not bothered in any way; no supplemental feeding was done. But after five years the whitetail population was still only six while the sikas had increased to thirty-two! After eight years biologists counted only three whitetails and sixty-two sikas—a tenfold increase in the aliens. By early 1979 the last of the native whitetails died, in a habitat virtually devastated by competitors. Conservation history has taught us over and over again that transplanting alien creatures to a new environment seldom works out in the long run. This was just one more confirmation of this truism.

I have seen many kinds of horned and antlered males

Spotted or axis deer (pictured), and sika deer, both natives of Asia, have been released and are now abundant on many Texas ranches. Almost everywhere the introduction has resulted in sharply diminishing numbers of whitetails that are unable to compete for the available food supply.

fight both during the rut and for dominance and over food. But never had I seen any fight more savagely, more noisily, or longer without flinching than two Shansi sika bucks on an Alberta ranch. Maybe some of this fury and determination, as well as their background in a cold land, makes it possible for sikas to endure the bitter winters and deep snows that other exotic deer cannot. Besides Texas, sikas are now thriving in several eastern shore counties of Maryland.

Fallow Deer

Time has practically erased the true origin of the fallow deer, *Dama dama*, a third very popular exotic introduced into America. It may have come from the Mediterranean or Middle East areas where no fallow deer live today in the wild. But because they are such attractive animals, with massive palmate antlers for the modest size of the males, they have more than managed to survive into the twentieth century on royal European hunting preserves. Now they are also living free in parts of Kentucky, California, and Maryland, as well as widely across Texas.

Probably no other mammal of the world comes in so many color variations as this species. The so-called typical fallow deer is fawn-colored with white spots in summer, changing to gray-brown or even mouse-colored in winter. We've seen herds of all-white and all-black fallows. There are also pintos, brown-spotted, even cream and silver-blue individuals, all of which have resulted from selective breeding for centuries in game parks and captive collections.

Antler conformation of fallow bucks falls somewhere between a moose and a mule deer. But I have always been struck more by the innate wildness of the species than by the impressive racks. The same docile animal of deer parks and petting zoos quickly reverts into a creature as shy and elusive as a whitetail soon after it is freed. The fallow ruts in mid-autumn in America, and the bucks become very vocal at that time. Their grunts can be heard a long distance away, but seeing them roar is another matter altogether.

Sambar and Pere David's Deer

The sambar deer, *Cervus unicolor*, of India, Burma, and Sri Lanka, is another deer that has found a home in the New World. Its popularity may be limited more by comparatively small trophy antlers, even on the finest bulls, than by the ability to adapt, as they have in parts of northwestern Florida. Red deer of northern Eurasia, *Cervus elaphus*, now live and proliferate on Texas ranchlands, where they readily interbreed with native American elk, from which the species is almost indistinguishable. A few swamp and brow-antlered deer, *Cervus eldi*, from India can also be found in the United States beyond the bars of zoos.

.Maybe the most interesting and still a rare alien is Pere David's deer, *Elaphurus davidianus*, which has not lived wild anywhere for more than two hundred years, until now. In fact its very existence was unknown until about 1865 when Abbe Armand David, an itinerant French missionary-naturalist, happened to spot them behind a wall of the imperial hunting preserve near Peking, China. This sanctuary was forbidden to both peasants and outsiders. Pere David realized he was looking at deer different than any known to science, and somehow he contrived to have a few live specimens shipped back to Europe.

China suffered from a terrible famine in 1894 and this was followed by torrential rains that flooded the Hun Ho River and devastated the Peking hunting preserve. Starving peasants quickly slaughtered and ate all the deer as they escaped. But those in Europe had multiplied, and in 1964 four were shipped back to China for a second chance at survival.

Pere David's deer also live in semicaptivity in at least three places in the United States, and maybe their release on a Texas ranch is one way to save a fascinating and gravely endangered species otherwise doomed on earth. In addition, there are some other Asian deer that are in serious trouble in their natural haunts. However the prospect of too many alien deer in the United States, not properly managed, is almost as threatening as is their extinction.

All photos: *Fallow deer, imports from the Middle East and possibly southern Europe, are established in whitetail country in a number of U.S. locations. The bucks, which have palmate antlers, are very shy. Fallow deer are direct range competitors with our native deer.*

Left: *The red deer of Eurasia lives free on a number of Texas ranches where it often hybridizes with American elk that are also introduced there.* **Overleaf:** *Pere David's deer, a native of China and once nearly extinct, is now living in a few protected, scattered whitetail habitats in the United States.*

CONSERVATION AND THE FUTURE

A LOVED—AND LOATHED?—ANIMAL

As early as 1877 naturalist-sportsman and Illinois Supreme Court justice John Caton wrote: "He who would enjoy the full measure of the outdoors must have a good knowledge of the natural history of creatures, and the more complete that knowledge, the more complete will be his enjoyment."

Since then probably no creature on earth has been more thoroughly studied, dissected, hunted, and observed than the whitetailed deer. The species had been the main justification for setting up field research stations in many states, and the money spent in the United States on deer study to date runs well into eight figures. It is possible that more wildlife biologists in the United States today are researching every aspect of the whitetailed deer than are studying all other wild species put together. If that seems to be an unwarranted emphasis on just one creature, it must be blamed on—or credited to—the immense importance of whitetails economically as *the* prime game animal of our times.

Not only does every one of the ten million North American deer hunters have to buy a hunting license (of which some money pays for the scientific wildlife studies), but he also travels far to hunt. He buys firearms and ammunition, on which there is a federal excise tax also used for wildlife conservation, special clothing and camping gear, food, fuel, vehicles, guide fees, everything from snacks to sunglasses just to go deer hunting, a growth industry almost everywhere for the last half-century.

So all of the field studies, the research work, and all the game management that resulted from all these studies may be largely responsible for the highest ever population of whitetailed deer in the United States. In 1986 biologist Mike Reagan of the Texas Parks and Wildlife Department claimed that 4.2 million whitetails (a state record for the species) and 10 to 20 percent of the North American population made Texas the nation's number one deer state. It also made the state a lot of money at a time when such other industries as oil and agriculture were not faring very well. In fact, deer are proving to be a much more valuable crop than livestock or row crops on many Texas ranches. The 1990s promise to be the Golden Age of the Whitetail.

Not all citizens are thrilled about the whitetail success story in the United States. Almost wherever suburbs have expanded outward from large eastern cities into "the country," deer have become a definite nuisance. They thrive on the bonanza of fresh garden vegetables, azaleas, yew, tulips, arborvitae, and hundreds of other goodies that weekend landscapers and horticulturists provide. The whitetails seem to sense that shooting is unsafe in most of suburbia and that most of the new suburbanites are against hunting anyway. As a result the annual deer damage is so high it is difficult to calculate. Fences lower than eight feet high are no barriers, and no repellents so far tested have proved effective. In addition, some of those invading deer are bearers of Lyme disease.

During 1992, deer-caused crop damage in just one state, New Jersey, was estimated at $20 million; in Pennsylvania at $30 million. At the same time there were 46,000 deer-vehicle

The sun sets on—or behind—a Texas buck, but not on the species, which is doing very well in almost every part of its vast range.

accidents in Michigan, mostly in densely settled areas. The average vehicle damage was calculated at $2,000 each. In 1992 more than 1,500 deer were living on the Gettysburg National Historical Park in southern Pennsylvania, an area that should support only one hundred. Fire Island National Seashore, New York, is besieged with a plague of whitetails that wander everywhere. At 14,000-acre Indiana Dunes National Lakeshore, along Lake Michigan's Indiana shore, a herd of twenty-nine grew to 350 in five years. These are only scattered examples, and it is understandable that in many highly populated areas deer are regarded as an epidemic rather than attractive wild creatures. Today there is a desperate need for some new device or strategy or substance (such as for selective birth control) to deal with this problem, which can only get worse.

THE WHITETAIL'S FUTURE

But what of the future elsewhere, in rural United States and Canada? Can the deer herd still continue to grow? Should it keep growing? There are good indications both that the upward spiral can last for a while and also that it cannot.

What Affects the Quality of the Habitat?

Deer populations have the potential for very rapid growth. At the same time there are natural limits to the number of deer that a parcel of real estate, of habitat, can support. These limits are determined by the quantity and quality of deer forage, plus the availability of winter habitat. The number of deer that an area can support in good physical condition over an extended period of time is known as the Biological Carrying Capacity (BCC), expressed as so many animals per square mile. Deer productivity always causes populations to exceed the BCC unless balanced by mortality—by predation or hunting. The bottom line is that when the BCC is exceeded, the quality of the habitat declines and so does the health of the deer.

Quality habitat is the key: Wherever we can maintain plenty of suitable whitetail habitat we will also have plenty of healthy deer. Where the habitat deteriorates, or worse, is paved over by condos, shopping centers, factories, or other human development, our whitetails will disappear. Serious research during the past few decades has enabled us to better evaluate habitat as well as to improve it. Although we have both the knowledge and the means to sustain excellent deer habitat all across the country, our overall conservation record has not always been a matter of pride. "Progress" at any cost usually comes first.

In the northeastern United States, especially in New En-

The antlers of deer, discarded or dropped in winter, do not remain intact long on the forest floor. Porcupines and smaller rodent species eat them. Even whitetails have been observed nibbling on whitetail antlers.

gland, virgin woodlands were cut long ago and the land cleared of native cover for farming. All too quickly, high-tech agricultural practices left little land unused and little left over for the whitetail. Deer disappeared. But in recent years a lot of the farmland has been abandoned to bush and second growth, which happens to be ideal for deer; so ideal that there now exists a genuine bonanza in whitetails. However there may be serious new trouble ahead in that northeastern region. The same acid rain that politicians and too many people choose to ignore, but which is subtly but surely killing lakes and ponds, is also beginning to blight vegetation, the same vegetation that deer and all creatures need to live.

In the northern Midwest and the Southeast some of today's forestry practices, especially the principle of sustained yield of timber products and of multiple use (that is, recreation and watershed management as well as timber harvest), have contributed to the present high deer numbers there. Since tall, mature forest with little undergrowth is poor whitetail habitat, any kind of logging or pulpwood cutting that retains some trees but allows sunlight to nourish undergrowth will be beneficial to deer. The future of the herds may be brightest in such situations. But there is an ugly trend now to cut down forests right to bare ground with monster equipment.

Arguably, whitetails on the farmlands in the heart of America and southern Canada may face the most uncertain future. The wild animals thrive best during the bad times, in depressed economic periods when some lands lie fallow and marginal acreage is allowed to revert to bush where it really belongs anyway. When world grain prices soar, wildlife habitat suffers in direct ratio as marginal land is plowed.

What is really an ominous development for whitetails in the central United States is big farming—agribusiness where the cropfields are the size of townships, where brush and woodlots are like warts on fair skin, and where the entire landscape is repeatedly sprayed or dusted with chemicals that are as potentially lethal to humans as they are to deer. The full results are not yet tabulated, but investigations underway are beginning to show that some of the same herbicides and pesticides that have rendered farming a very risky, cancer-threatening occupation in Iowa and the Dakotas can also cause deformities and affect the normal behavior of deer. Often in the past wildlife research has uncovered facts, which when put to use can improve or even save human lives. They may be among the most important discoveries of all.

Although whitetails are not affected nearly as much as are mule deer and elk by excessive grazing of livestock on public lands of the West—on national forests, national wild-

Few animals are better named. Far too often the white tail, is the first, last, and only part of this species we ever glimpse.

life refuges, and Bureau of Land Management property—there are some areas where whitetails also suffer. The species simply is not compatible with sheep grazing, historically a damaging (to the environment) practice worldwide. Some modern sheep ranching on well-managed rangeland is not necessarily destructive, but great areas of the Old World have been reduced to deserts or near-deserts by centuries of sheep grazing. U.S. public lands are also suffering as a result of it.

Deer Management

In recent years many Texas ranchers have been the first to realize that one way to better, healthier, and more profitable whitetailed deer herds (and to higher incomes for themselves) was by reducing domestic livestock numbers in favor of deer. In fact a whole new profession of scientifically trained ranch wildlife managers has originated in the state. Today a large corps of wildlife and deer biologists is employed full time to manage many larger Texas spreads, while smaller ranches hire freelance biologists on a seasonal basis or as advisors.

During the past generation, at the same time whitetailed deer study has increased, so have new techniques. New tools have also been devised. In fact today's efficient live-capturing of large wild animals was developed by a deer biologist in Georgia during the 1950s. Since then thousands of deer have been immobilized by firing darts filled with muscle relaxing drugs from guns into the deer. When the drug enters the animal's bloodstream, the deer is tranquilized long enough for researchers to make a thorough examination, teeth to tail, and to permanently mark the creature. Marking is done by a variety of methods including ear tagging (with a metal or plastic tag), by tattooing, with brightly colored streamers, and by attaching radio transmitter collars.

Being able to mark and so identify thousands of deer nationwide has resulted in a vast reservoir of valuable information. The radio collars—and radio telemetry—have made it possible for a game manager to follow a deer's movements wherever it wanders and to locate it exactly at any given time. The deer's travel range, what it eats, how long it lives, and how it dies can be accurately determined. Just the return of ear tags from deer taken by hunters has provided a mountain of information about this valuable species.

The crop of young, vigorous, innovative game biologists graduating from dozens of state and provincial universities has increased our knowledge of deer more than can be quickly calculated. Computers have helped them evaluate the mass of deer information already on hand. But another modern instrument, the small, maneuverable helicopter, has enabled biologists to more accurately census deer and other big game than was ever possible before. The choppers also make it possible to capture alive specific deer, rather than the first one to stroll down a trail, and even to move deer from one study area to the next.

One warm morning during an aerial census in September I rode in a helicopter across a ranch with which I was already familiar. But what I saw from that unfamiliar, overhead angle was astonishing. To begin, I counted about twice as many deer, maybe more, than I would have been able to see by any ground census. Second, we spotted a number of male deer with the outrageously large antlers one only sees in calendar paintings. No doubt about it; there were record-book bucks here that we would not otherwise have known about.

Understandably much of today's research, especially in Texas, is now being devoted to raising bucks with the largest possible trophy antlers rather than to producing large or larger numbers of deer. Nowadays growing numbers of hunters are no longer willing to just take a buck—any buck. They want a rack they can brag about and they are willing to pay for it. So ranchers with their biologist allies are engaged in an all-out competition to develop a race of trophy deer, a race that is not without negative implications.

Some of this effort toward bigger bucks is going into supplemental feeding of grains and mixes especially concocted with those minerals necessary for optimum antler growth. The jury is still out, however, on exactly how much can be accomplished by nutrition alone. Wherever possible or affordable (and sometimes the sky's the limit), the greatest emphasis has been placed on selective breeding. The first step is to acquire big trophy bucks. These studs may be imported from some other part of the country and are bred under controlled conditions to does also born of good stock. Some such programs

seem to be paying off.

Another technique is to carefully cull the deer of a herd both to eliminate animals of inferior size or health, and to maintain the total herd size at well below the carrying capacity of the ranch. That way a few special deer can have all, or almost all, of the best natural foods, rather than having to compete with many other deer for nutrition. Another aim is to keep the ratio of bucks to does about even, one to one, rather than many females per every buck, which is usually the case. "Spike" bucks are culled because spikes, antlers bearing one tine or point per side, are an early indication of low potential antler growth in the future, no matter what the reason.

Of course all of this management costs plenty of money. It usually also requires some very elaborate breeding facilities, not unlike those in the animal husbandry laboratories at large universities. The demand for whitetail trophies today seems to more than justify it. In addition to Canadian and American sportspeople, more and more hunters are now coming from Europe and Japan for something outstanding to decorate their own trophy rooms.

On a less lofty, less costly level, it is possible today for individual landowners, or small farmers and hobbyists, to improve both the health and numbers of whitetailed deer on smaller tracts anywhere in America. Selective breeding and regulated harvests may be out of the question because, in the United States, these are controlled by the various states with a statewide deer management program. But there is nothing to prevent a landowner from enhancing his acreage for deer by planting certain crops with whitetails either partially or specifically in mind. Deer are especially partial to plots of turnips or rutabagas left unharvested. Deer do at times wander far in search of food, but generally tend to spend almost their entire lives in limited core territories. Many game managers are now convinced that deer can be kept pretty much in a home area, on one farm, if their food needs are somehow provided. Research is still ongoing about the best ways to do this regionally.

According to Larry Weishuhn, a well-known Uvalde, Texas, deer consultant, sowing numerous small plots of deer food on a ranch or farm is a good, not-too-expensive way to

Overleaf: In recent years, deer populations have increased beyond the Biological Carrying Capacity (BCC) of their ranges to an abundance not in their own best interests. This photo was made on a tree plantation that was planted for pulpwood in south Georgia where artificial feeding attracts herds of deer.

148

go. Mixtures of oats and clover planted in the fall are what he recommends. Wheat may grow better locally and even be better nutritionally, but in some areas, whitetails still prefer the oats and clover or alfalfa, left uncut. Weishuhn advises having soil samples analyzed and then fertilizing the deer plots accordingly if the soil does not assay rich enough. Many tests have shown that whitetails will invariably feed in a fertilized field, but ignore exactly the same kind of food plot right next to it which has not been treated.

When planning deer plots, long and narrow strips next to trees or heavy brush for handy cover offer security and resting places for deer in addition to the food. Plowing under good natural deer foods just to make a deer plot should be avoided. If livestock share the land, every deer plot must be enclosed with a four-foot fence that cattle cannot jump, but that whitetails can clear with feet to spare.

Inevitably, knowledge of the best ways to plant for deer or to improve deer habitat are beginning to come out of a computer. Progressive biologists such as Aaron Moen of Cornell University in New York are now feeding past decades of research material into their computers and are coming up with important results, some of them surprising. Such information as the ideal carrying capacity of any deer range and how many deer must be harvested annually to keep the range in prime condition, or to even improve it, is now available. According to Moen, the time has come when we can no longer afford to make important conservation decisions such as the length and scope of an open hunting season on the basis of guesswork, emotion, on political or commercial pressures. We can now do better than that.

Computer-in-biology pioneer Moen believes that we have a social responsibility not only to provide habitat for North America's most popular deer, but also to keep deer populations under control. That is now a widespread problem and so far hunting is the only practical way to solve it.

A nagging concern that seemingly will not go away is the inability of outdoorspeople to really understand the complex relationship between whitetails and their habitat. Too many hunters go afield, hoping or expecting to find deer behind every tree, without understanding why whitetail numbers are high or low. They should know that when given full protection, or when just bucks are hunted for a ten-year period, a herd of a thousand deer can multiply to twenty thousand! The effect on the environment of such an increase would be disastrous. Abnormally high populations of deer cannot be sustained forever. So we *must* keep deer populations at very near to the carrying capacity of the range for their own good and for ours.

Until recently a good many deer managers have been reluctant to depend on computers to spit out answers to biological questions. But with less and less funding available and with less time left to calculate manually—the hard way, more deer researchers are finally turning to computers for the greater benefit of the deer.

From the very beginning, laws concerning deer (and other wildlife) have been based on myths, on politics or the lack of sound information that could be programmed into a computer. For example, as long ago as 1645, in an attempt to restore a then-dwindling population of whitetails, the Massachusetts Bay Colony offered a reward to anyone killing a wolf. This originated a bounty system on predators in North America that has cost taxpayers many millions of dollars in the three-plus centuries since, all of it ill-spent. We still wage war on coyotes in the mistaken belief that killing them will benefit our whitetailed deer. As we have seen before, native predators are usually a boon to the prey species.

Poaching

The downward slide in deer numbers from time to time has resulted in laws that outlawed the sale of venison, the export of deer hides, the shooting of does, and the use of hounds or certain arms in hunting; almost everything except attention to the deteriorating environment. Another strategy when deer are not doing well has always been to enact still tougher laws against poaching and to hire more game wardens.

Poaching is a sad, antisocial crime that has existed since the first closed season on deer (in Rhode Island in May 1646) was declared. And in today's social climate it may be a greater problem than ever before. A small amount of today's poaching, the illegal killing of deer, is for subsistence by poor people during hard times. But most is of a more ugly nature. From time to time, especially in the East and Midwest, organized poaching rings kill large numbers of deer, mostly at night, to sell the meat. Other poaching is simply thrill-killing, vandal-

Left: *The unnatural toll of deer is high every year, especially along our high-speed highways. Farm fences also take a toll. But the deer are prolific enough to maintain numbers, in spite of this and even with regular fall hunting seasons.* **Overleaf:** *The best times to observe deer anywhere are soon after dawn and again at dusk, when they are more likely to be in open places.*

ism, or something equally unexplainable.

Nearly all poachers are mainly after trophy racks, and this trophy poaching has boomed since the 1980s. In broad daylight along a road near Albany, New York, Paul Gallacchi poached a super twenty-four-point buck that scored 212 5/8 Boone & Crockett points. He was arrested, paid a $1,255 fine, and the antlers were confiscated. But the man said he would gladly pay that amount for another buck of similar size.

In Texas especially, a few poachers have been apprehended trespassing posted lands in the search of record-book heads for the thrill alone. One such hunter, Ronnie Carroll, became locally famous, a sort of folk hero in south Texas, for the way he wandered freely with a backpack, living off the land and defying massive police dragnets to catch him (until 1982), just to shoot a bigger buck than anybody else. But most of the trophy poachers are in the single-minded search of heads they can sell. Any whitetail rack scoring high enough to make the Boone & Crockett record book would be worth at least $10,000 on the illegal market in the early 1990s.

Deplorable as it is, poaching has never had more than a temporary, if any noticeable effect at all, on whitetailed deer populations across America. Sufficient deer habitat of high quality remains the key to the future. Although the smallest member of the deer family in North America, the whitetail is a tough, adaptable, prolific species, far more at the mercy of bulldozers and chemicals, of politicians, folklore, and indifference than of all the poachers put together. Right now its future is much brighter than that of many other creatures sharing the whitetail's beautiful world.

Above: *Deer can be a special nuisance in winter when, hard pressed for food in the wild, they enter suburban gardens to feed on domestic plants and ornamentals.* **Right:** *Whitetails are not beloved and welcome everywhere. Suburbanites especially do not appreciate their invasions into gardens and backyards as here, when wild food supplies run low.*

153

References and Suggested Readings

The following are good sources for more information on deer.

Bauer, Erwin. *Deer in Their World*. Outdoor Life Books, New York, 1990.

Bauer, Erwin. *Horned and Antlered Game*. Outdoor Life Books, New York, 1986.

Bauer, Erwin, and Peggy Bauer. *Photographing Wild Texas*. University of Texas Press, Austin, TX, 1985.

Boone & Crockett Club. *Records of North American Whitetail Deer*. Falcon Press, Helena, MT, 1991.

Brothers, Al, and Murphy E. Ray, Jr. *Producing Quality Whitetails*. Wildlife Services Publications, Laredo, TX, 1975.

Brown, Robert D., editor. *Antler Development in Cervidae*. Texas A&I University, Kingsville, TX, 1986.

Dahlberg, Burton, and Ralph Guettinger. *The Whitetailed Deer in Wisconsin*. Wisconsin Conservation Department, Madison, WI, 1956.

Goss, Richard. *Deer Antlers: Regeneration, Function & Evolution*. Academic Press, Orlando, FL, 1989.

Laycock, George. *Whitetail*. W. W. Norton Company, New York, 1966.

Mattis, George. *Whitetail Fundamentals*. World Publishing, New York, 1969.

Madson, John, and others. *Outdoor Life Deer Hunter's Encyclopedia*. Outdoor Life Books, New York, 1985.

Putman, Rory. *The Natural History of Deer*. Cornell University Press, Ithaca, NY, 1988.

Rogers, Robert, editor. *Professional's Guide to Whitetails*. Texas Hunting Services, Corpus Christi, TX, 1984.

Rogers, Robert. *Great Whitetails of North America*. Texas Hunting Services, Corpus Christi, TX, 1981.

Rue, Leonard Lee III. *The Deer of North America*. Outdoor Life—Crown Publishers, New York, 1978.

Thornberry, Russell. *Trophy Deer of Alberta*. Greenhorn Publishing, Rocky Mountain House, Alberta, 1982.

Wegner, Rob. *Bibliography on Deer and Deer Hunting: A Comprehensive Annotated Compilation of Books in English Pertaining to Deer and Their Hunting*. Watkins Natural History Books, Dolgeville, NY, 1991.

Whitehead, G. Kenneth. *Deer of the World*. Viking Press, New York, 1972.

Whitehead, G. Kenneth. *The Whitehead Encyclopedia of Deer*. Voyageur Press, Inc., Stillwater, MN, 1993.

Wildlife Management Institute. *White-Tailed Deer Ecology & Management*. Stackpole Books, Harrisburg, PA, 1984.

Wildlife Management Institute. *Big Game of North America*. Stackpole Books, Harrisburg, PA, 1978.

INDEX

Abundance, see Population
Antlers, 10, 62, 73–97
  age and, 84
  color of, 76
  conformation of, 78, 80, 84
  does with, 73
  drop points, 97
  growth of, 73–75, 80, 84
    nutrition and, 84
    weather and, 84
  heredity and, 80, 84
  horns compared to, 73
  locking of, 30
  non-typical, 73, 78, 84, 92
  pedicels and, 73, 75, 76
  purposes of, 80
  rattling of, 29, 32, 37
  recycling of, 76, 142
  rubbing of, 27
  scoring of, 92
    Boone & Crockett points, 90, 92
  shedding of, 30, 73, 76
  size of, 75, 80, 84
  see also Velvet
Autumn, 27–35
Axis deer (Axis axis), 130, 132

Behavior, 24, 59–71, 75
  age and, 66, 80
  during rut, 27, 29–30
    see also Fighting; Flehman
  habitat and, 61
  moon and, 64
  weather and, 61–64
Birth, 44–45
  first, 44
  multiple, 44
Blacktailed deer (Odocoileus hemionus columbainus and O.h. sitkensis), 123, 124
Body language, 64, 66
  see also Communication
Boone & Crockett Club, 92

Breeding, 30, 68
  first, 53
  see also Birth; Reproduction, high rate of
Brow-antlered deer (Cervus eldi), 134

Camouflage, 20
  of fawns, 45
Caribou (Rangifer tarandus), 129
Census, see Population
Color, see Physical characteristics, pelage
Communication, 22, 64, 66
  see also Body language; Vocalizations
Conservation and management of whitetail, 18, 141–152

Description, see Physical characteristics
Development, 61, 80
Diet, 35, 40, 52–53
  browsing, 40, 52–53, 55, 114
  see also Fawns, diet of
Digestion, 36, 53
  lipogenesis, 53
  rumination, 8, 53
Disease, 36, 67
Dominance, see Social hierarchy

Ears, 22, 94
  see also Hearing
Elk (Cervus canadensis), 124, 126
Embryo resorption, 40
Endurance, 8, 25, 53, 102–103, 152
Estrus, 27, 30, 66
  see also Breeding; Rut
Evolution, 8, 25
Exotics, 130, 132–134
  raising of, 132

Fallow deer (Dama dama), 133, 134
Fawns, 44–52
  bucks and, 47
  camouflage of, 45

development of, 45, 47, 75
diet of, 45
does and, 22, 36, 44–45, 47, 50, 52
  see also Nursing
mortality of, 36, 44, 45, 106, 118
scent of, 47
weaning of, 47
weight at birth, 45
Fighting, 59–61
  among bucks, 29–30, 59–61, 62, 76
  among does, 60
Flagging, see Tail
Flehman, 66, 69
Fur, see Physical characteristics, pelage

Gestation, 44
  see also Breeding
Growth, see Development

Habitat, 8, 10, 18, 61, 117, 142–143, 149
  threats to, 25, 47, 52, 142–143
Hearing, 22
Home range, 24
Humans and whitetails, 22, 24, 36, 45, 46, 66, 67–68, 71, 92, 141–152
  attacks on humans by whitetails, 68, 71
  crop damage, 53, 141–142
  historical importance of whitetail, 15, 18, 73, 92
  laws regarding whitetails, 141, 149
  poaching, 92, 94, 149, 152
  raising whitetails, 110, 113, 144–145
  supplemental feeding of whitetails, 36, 149
  see also Conservation and management of whitetails; Habitat, threats to; Hunting; Mortality, causes of; Photographing whitetails
Hunting, 18, 66, 67–68, 149
  seasons for, 67
  for trophy bucks, 84, 92, 94

Intelligence, 24

Leaping ability, 24
Lifespan, 52

Mortality, 40, 52
  causes of, 40, 44, 45, 52
    highway deaths, 52, 67, 141–142, 149
  rates of, 40
  see also Humans and whitetails, poaching; Hunting
Moose (*Alces alces*), 126–127, 128
Mule deer (*Odocoileus hemionus*), 18, 117, 122, 124
  compared to whitetail, 123–124
  interbreeding with whitetails, 123

Nursing, 45
Nutrition, see Diet

Odocoileus virginianus virginianus, 8
O.v. borealis, 8
O.v. carminis, 15
O. v. clavium, 8
O.v. couesi, 20, 92
O.v. leucurus, 20
O.v. macrourus, 8, 15
O.v. texanus, 7, 15

Parasites, 36, 67, 70
Pedicels, see Antlers, pedicels and
Pelage, see Physical appearance, pelage
Pere David's deer (*Elaphurus davidianus*), 134, 137
Photographing whitetails, 29, 32
  attracting whitetails for, 7, 32, 37
  blinds for, 7
Photoperiodism, 27
Physical characteristics, 8, 18–24
  age and, 18, 20
  pelage, 20–22, 44, 53
  size, 18, 20, 94, 123

northern vs. southern whitetails, 8, 20
trophy bucks, see Trophy bucks
weight, 18, 20
see also Antlers; Ears; Fawns, development of; Rut, physical changes during; Tail; Teeth
Play, 59–61
  among adults, 59
  among fawns, 59
Poaching, see Humans and whitetails, poaching
Populations, 8, 67–68, 141, 149, 152
Predators, 45, 64, 99, 113
  black bear, 106
  bobcat, 106, 110
  cougar, 99, 105, 106, 108, 113
  coyote, 103, 105, 106
  dog (domestic), 64, 106
  hog (feral), 117, 118
  wolf, 99, 102–103
Prenatal behavior, 36, 40

Range, 8, 10, 15, 18, 123, 129
  carrying capacity, 40, 106
  map, 9
Red deer (*Cervus elaphus*), 133–134, 137
Reproduction, high rate of, 24, 68, 142
Running, 24–25
  gaits, 24–25
  speed, 24–25
Rut, 7–8, 27–32
  length of season, 32
  physical changes during, 27
  see also Behavior, during rut; Breeding; Photoperiodism

Sambar deer (*Cervus unicolor*), 133
Scraping, 27, 29
Shyness, 25, 29, 32, 66
Sika deer, 132–133
Size, see Physical characteristics, size

Sleep, 64
Smell, sense of, 8, 22, 64
Social hierarchy, 76, 80
Speed, see Running, speed
Subspecies, 8, 10
  see also specific subspecies
Summer, 76
Survival, adaptations for, 8, 22, 24, 47, 61, 102
  escape ability, 24–25
  instincts, 36, 64
  stealth, 24
Swimming, 102, 113

Tail, 22, 66
Tarsal glands, 22, 27, 47
Taxonomy, 8, 15
Teeth, 52
  age and, 20
Tracks, 8, 24
Tracking whitetails, 24
Territory, 24, 29, 145
  see also Home range
Trophy bucks, 84, 92, 94, 152
  see also Antlers, scoring of

Velvet, 73–75, 76
Vision, 22, 24, 64
Vocalizations, 8, 22

Wapiti, see Elk
Weight, see Physical characteristics, weight
Winter, 35–36, 40–41, 44–45
  "hunger moon," 35, 47

Yards, 35, 36, 40
  see also Winter
Young, see Fawns

ABOUT THE AUTHORS

Erwin and Peggy Bauer are busy, full-time photographers and writers of travel, adventure, and environmental subjects. Based in Paradise Valley, Montana, the Bauers have specialized in photographing wildlife worldwide for over forty years. Their images come from the Arctic to the Antarctic; Borneo to Brazil: Africa; India; and remote places you may never have heard of.

The Bauers' recent magazine credits include *Natural History*, *Outdoor Life*, *Audubon*, *National Geographic*, *Smithsonian*, *Wildlife Conservation*, *National Wildlife* and *International Wild-life*, *Sierra*, *Safari*, *Sports Afield*, *Bugle*, *Petersen's Hunting*, and *Western Outdoors*. Their photographs annually illustrate the calendars of the Sierra Club, the Audubon Society, World Wildlife Fund, and others. The Bauers have a dozen books currently in print including *Yellowstone*, published by Voyageur Press, and another, *Wild Africa*, in production. The couple has won awards for wildlife photography in national and international competitions. Erwin and Peggy Bauer may be the most frequently published wildlife photographers in the world today.